B L U E P R I N T S
Easter

Joy A Palmer

Stanley Thornes (Publishers) Ltd

Do you receive *BLUEPRINTS NEWS*?

Blueprints is an expanding series of practical teacher's ideas books and photocopiable resources for use in primary schools. Books are available for separate infant and junior age ranges for every core and foundation subject, as well as for an ever widening range of other primary teaching needs. These include **Blueprints Primary English** books and **Blueprints Resource Banks**. **Blueprints** are carefully structured around the demands of National Curriculum in England and Wales, but are used successfully by schools and teachers in Scotland, Northern Ireland and elsewhere.

Blueprints provide :

- Total curriculum coverage
- Hundreds of practical ideas
- Books specifically for the age range you teach
- Flexible resources for the whole school or for individual teachers
- Excellent photocopiable sheets - ideal for assessment and children's work profiles
- Supreme value

Books may be bought by credit card over the telephone and information obtained on **(0242) 228888**. Alternatively, photocopy and return this **FREEPOST** form to receive **Blueprints News**, our regular update on all new and existing titles. You may also like to add the name of a friend who would be interested in being on the mailing list.

Please add my name to the **BLUEPRINTS NEWS** mailing list.

Mr/Mrs/Miss/Ms --

Home address --

---Postcode ------------------------

School address --

-- Postcode ------------------------

Please also send **BLUEPRINTS NEWS** to :

Mr/Mrs/Miss/Ms --

Address --

-- Postcode ------------------------

To: Marketing Services Dept., Stanley Thornes Ltd, FREEPOST (GR 782), Cheltenham, GL50 1BR

First published in 1995 by:
Stanley Thornes (Publishers) Ltd
Ellenborough House
Wellington Street
CHELTENHAM GL50 1YD
England

A catalogue record for this book is available from the British Library.

ISBN 0–7487–1813–5

Typeset by Tech-Set, Gateshead, Tyne & Wear.
Printed in Great Britain at The Bath Press, Avon.

CONTENTS

Introduction   iv

Section 1: Three Topics for Easter
            Eastertime   3
            Eggs   21
            Life cycles   38

Section 2: Services and Assemblies
            Trees: An Easter assembly   59
            The Easter story   66

Section 3: Templates, Timesavers, Activities, Resources
            Templates   73
            Eastertime fun   91
            Easter legends and customs   103
            Information and resources   107

INTRODUCTION

This book provides a wealth of information, ideas and practical suggestions for teaching and learning about the festival of Easter and related topics. It is aimed at teachers and pupils of both Key Stages 1 and 2. No attempt has been made to match activities and resource material to precise pupil ages and levels of learning: you are invited to 'dip into' the extensive material provided, and adopt and adapt suggestions to suit the needs of individuals and class situations.

Blueprints *Easter* is divided into three main sections. Section 1 consists of material relating to three topics: **Eastertime**, **Eggs** and **Life cycles**. The pages devoted to each of these topics contain teacher resource material and suggestions of activities for pupils organised under subject areas of the National Curriculum, plus six photocopiable pupil sheets which are cross-referenced with the teacher material. These three topics are designed to be pursued in their own right as cross-curricular projects for study in the weeks of term leading up to Eastertime; alternatively, this material can be 'mixed and matched' as inevitably there is a degree of overlap between certain aspects of their content. It should also be pointed out that the Christian story of Easter is contained within the **Eastertime** topic, and is also to be found in a different form in Section 2 of the book.

Section 2 provides suggested outline texts for two class or school services or assemblies, which can be performed in the Easter season. One is closely linked to the Christian story of Easter; the other is a thematic service on the subject of trees, telling of the key trees mentioned in the events of the first Easter. Both contain examples of pupils' own writing which could be adapted for use or may provide a stimulus for helping your own pupils to compose passages of creative writing suitable for inclusion in the services.

Section 3 of the book consists of a wealth of useful photocopiable sheets: templates, timesavers, activities and resources, including further material about a number of well-known Easter customs and traditions, together with suggestions for further reading and other sources of information.

As a whole, **Blueprints** *Easter* offers an extensive range of teacher and pupil material that can be utilised year after year as different aspects of the Easter season are focused upon. Inevitably there is an emphasis on the Christian story of Easter, alongside interpretations of related springtime themes. The book aims to give both teachers and pupils an overview of information and opportunity for in-depth studies of the religious, the legendary, the scientific, the serious and the joyous aspects of the Easter festival. Have fun at Eastertime!

Acknowledgements
The author is most grateful to Joyce Palmer of Sutton Coldfield, England, for her well tried and tested ideas for Easter cards contained on pages 7–9 within the **Eastertime** topic; also to Min Moxon of Los Altos, California, for information on the tradition of dyeing hard-boiled eggs (pp. 91). The poster on the 'Easter Egg Hunt' (pp. 90 and 106) is adapted from an original designed and sponsored by the Los Altos Village Association, California, USA.

SECTION 1
Three Topics for Easter

Eastertime

English

- Meaning of 'Easter
- The goddess Eostre
- Lent denial and sacrifice
- Ideas for self-improvement
- Easter customs and traditions
- Paschal frieze
- Easter poems
- Palm Sunday – feelings of a donkey
- Origins of Easter bunny
- Easter puzzle
- Egg sayings and rhymes
- Symbols of Easter
- Contrasting poems – despair and rejoicing

Art

- Stained-glass window pictures
- Make Easter cards
- Make Easter bonnets
- Rabbit party invitations
- Egg patterns
- Egg-shell rabbits
- Decorate egg insides
- Easter baskets
- Wool pompom chicks
- Make an egg tree
- Egg hunt pictures
- Paintings of the Easter story

Geography

- Easter around the world

EASTERTIME cross-curricular links

Music

- Music, songs and hymns of Easter

RE

- Diary of the Easter season
- The Christian story of Easter
- Compare the Gospel stories
- News reports of Easter

Science

- Passage of the seasons — spring equinox
- Dates of Easter
- Easter sunrise
- Grow an Easter garden

ENGLISH

Activity 1: What does 'Easter' mean?

A Research the meaning of the word 'Easter'. It is thought to derive from the word 'Oster', meaning 'to rise'; also from the name Eostre or Osterr, goddess of dawn and of spring, who was worshipped by the Anglo-Saxons around the time of the vernal equinox (see **Science** activities). Consult reference books to discover more about festivals that were held in honour of Eostre.

B Use **Copymaster 1** (Eostre) as a stimulus for further discussion and writing on this subject. The copymaster shows an artist's impression of the goddess. Talk about the content of this picture, pointing out the relevant signs of springtime. Children will enjoy colouring the figure and decorating the sheet. Ask them to produce accompanying writing about pagan March festivals in honour of Eostre, or perhaps to compile prayers to the goddess asking her to bring the spring.

C Help the children to appreciate that Easter means different things to different people. In modern times, rather like Christmas, the Easter festival is a mixture of religious and non-religious celebrations. It is a festival in which a deeply religious story central to the Christian Church is interwoven with pagan customs, traditions, fun and games aimed at celebrating the arrival of spring. This activity could be developed by going around the class in a 'brainstorming' session, asking the children to say something about the meaning of Easter. Key ideas could then be written as sentences for display on the classroom wall. Create an artistic display for this purpose, such as words in Easter eggs, for example:

Activity 2: Sacrifice and self-improvement at Easter

A Link Easter to the season of Lent (see **RE** activities) and devise activities around the themes of denial or of improving ourselves. For example, provide a list of 'goodies' and ask the children to decide which would be the greatest sacrifice for them, for example:

Put a ring around the 3 things that would be the hardest to give up . . .

B Along similar lines, ask pupils to write about 'The greatest sacrifice', explaining what they would find hardest to give up and why. This could be restricted to edible things, or could include pastimes such as television, computer games and sport.

C Discuss why 'self-improvement' is a good idea. Make a list of reasons why we should work hard at this: for example, we may have more friends, we may do better at school, we may like ourselves better, we may have other rewards.

Activity 3: Easter customs and traditions

A Research various customs and traditions associated with the Easter season, such as the wearing of new clothes on Easter Sunday. An old country rhyme warned that new clothes should be worn:

At Easter let your clothes be new,
Or else, be sure, you will it rue.

Note See also Section 3 of this book for further information about Easter customs and traditions.

Background information
The custom of 'pace-egging' is described on p. 104. The decoration of eggs is not included in this topic, as it is an activity described in the forthcoming topic on **Eggs**. Its origins, however, are relevant to both topics. Hard-boiled eggs with decorated shells were known as 'pace-eggs'. The word 'pace' comes from 'paschal', which is another name for Easter. Eggs were a forbidden food during Lent, which is why they featured strongly in Easter celebrations – as foods, decorations, and in games.

B Make a paschal frieze, displaying writing about ancient customs and traditions of Eastertime, and with a colourful border of pace-eggs.

Organise a classroom display of work on the theme of Easter

Activity 4: Easter poetry

[A] Read poems which have been written about Easter and discuss their meaning: for example, 'He Is Risen' by C.F. Alexander, 'The World Itself Keeps Easter Day' by J.M. Neale, 'The Donkey' by G.K. Chesterton (all in the book *Times Delights* by R. Wilson, published by Beaver Books, 1977); and 'An Easter Chick' by Thirza Wakley, 'When Mary thro' the Garden Went' by Mary E. Coleridge, 'Easter Praise' by Rodney Bennett (all in *The Book of a Thousand Poems*, published by Bell and Hyman, 1983).

[B] Use the poem 'The Donkey' by G.K. Chesterton as a basis for discussion and art work about the glorious entry of Jesus into Jerusalem on the first Palm Sunday. The words of the last verse are printed on **Copymaster 2** (Palm Sunday). Talk about why the donkey was chosen by Jesus (notably because donkeys were a sign of peace) and suggest that the children complete the copymaster by drawing Jesus on his donkey, with crowds of people waving palms in the background. They could then undertake their own creative writing about this day, or try to express the feelings of the donkey at the centre of the activity.

[C] Tell the children the origins of the Easter bunny (see p.104). Suggest that they write and illustrate stories about Easter rabbits, such as 'Hiding places', telling of where bunny hides his eggs to be found on Easter morning, or 'Rabbits' tea party', telling of an imaginary Easter party attended by a rabbit family.

Activity 5: An Easter puzzle

Use **Copymaster 3** (Easter puzzle) to help children learn words associated with Eastertime. This will appeal to younger children as well as older ones as the clues are in pictorial rather than written form. Pictures can be coloured when the puzzle is complete.

Background information
Answers to Copymaster 3 are:

Across	Down
1. Rabbit	1. Eostre
2. Chicks	2. Paschal candle
3. Church	3. Eggs
4. Lilies	
5. Sunrise	

Activity 6: All about eggs

[A] Make a study of sayings about eggs. Ask the children to conduct their own research, asking parents and friends if they know any riddles, maxims or rhymes, etc., then write them out. An illustrated display can go alongside decorated eggs. The following will form a useful start for learning and discussion:

Riddle
What has neither head nor foot,
Neither arms nor tail?
What is neither living nor dead?
(Answer: An egg.)

Sayings
Don't put all your eggs in one basket.
Don't count your chickens before they're hatched.

Rhyme
Humpty Dumpty sat on a wall,
Humpty Dumpty had a great fall.
All the King's horses and all the King's men
Couldn't put Humpty together again.

Note Many ideas about eggs will be found in the **Eggs** topic in this book.

Activity 7: Symbols of Easter

Investigate well-known symbols of Easter. Ask the children to make suggestions about these, then design a border for one of your Easter friezes incorporating appropriate symbols. These may include flowers, lambs, rabbits, the cross (symbol of the Christian religion), the lily (often used to decorate churches at Eastertime, as the growth of the tall white flower is said to remind Christians of the way in which Jesus came back to life), eggs, chicks, and pussy-willow catkins (in some European countries these are picked especially for Easter). Ask the children which is their favourite Easter symbol, and to explain why, either in discussion or in writing.

Activity 8: Writing Easter poems

Ask children to write their own poems with two verses (or write two separate poems), the first to express the gloom and sadness of Good Friday, the second to portray the rejoicing and happiness that we associate with Easter Sunday. Suggest that they try to capture the great contrast between the atmosphere of these two days. In preparation for this, lists of words associated with both days could be drawn up:

GOOD FRIDAY	EASTER SUNDAY
death	
sadness	Alleluyah!
unhappiness	rejoicing
tragedy	happiness
misery	victory
suffering	triumph
anguish	resurrection
darkness	life
pain	hope
agony	beginnings
despair	joy
endings	celebration
mourning	singing
	love

GEOGRAPHY

Activity: Easter celebrations around the world

A Find out about how Easter is celebrated around the world: many countries have special customs and traditions. Use **Copymaster 4** (Easter around the world), in conjunction with the following background information and other reference material, to help pupils appreciate this. They can colour and match the national flags depicting six countries with the relevant traditions shown on the copymaster. When they have coloured the pictures and flags, pupils can select one country for further research, writing and illustration.

Background information
• In some states of the USA (California, for example) it is customary for adults to organise Easter egg hunts for the children. Eggs are hidden outdoors if the weather is warm and sunny, and children hunt around until they are found.
• Ham is a well-known Easter dish in many countries, including the USA and England. In Germany, a good luck greeting is '*Schwein haben!*', which literally means 'have a pig!'
• In Sweden, children celebrate Easter by drawing witches on pieces of paper and adding an Easter greeting. These are then delivered to friends by the children who dress up as witches. As they do this, firecrackers are set off in the streets. It is believed that the witches stand for bad luck, and so the firecrackers are lit to send this bad luck away.

• In Greece, Easter is celebrated with outdoor barbecues of meat, eggs, bread and salad. A splendid array of these foods is set up on long tables and large gatherings of families and friends get together.
• In Spain, people dance in the streets on Easter Sunday.
• In some parts of France and Italy, it is believed that four white horses pass by at Eastertime, pulling a chariot full of eggs.

B Using this information and supplementary research, organise a class frieze on 'Easter around the world', depicting a variety of colourful celebrations.

C Use the template in Section 3, p. 90 (Easter fun from afar – Los Altos, California) as a basis for discussion and further activity. This is an artist's impression of an authentic advertisement for a neighbourhood Easter hunt in Los Altos, in the southern San Francisco Bay area of California. Read the poster through with the children, informing them that this is an annual event in the town and typical of neighbourhoods in this part of the world, where Eastertime weather is usually warm and sunny and ideal for outdoor games. As well as colouring the poster, suggest that the children do imaginative art work and creative writing depicting the scene that the poster conjures up.

SCIENCE

Activity: The spring equinox

A Find out more about the passage of the seasons, and in particular the spring equinox, which is close to Eastertime. A useful source of information on this subject is **Blueprints** *Seasonal Topics* in this series, which has a wealth of suggested activities for the topic of springtime.

B Help the children to appreciate that Easter Sunday falls on a different day each year because the date of Easter depends on the cycle of the sun and the moon. It is therefore known as a 'moveable feast'.

Background information
Easter Sunday is the first day after the full moon which happens on or after 21 March (the spring or vernal equinox). If the full moon occurs on a Sunday, then Easter day is the Sunday after that. The date of Easter day always falls between 22 March and 25 April.

C Organise a class debate on the subject of 'A fixed Easter'. Some people hold strong views that Easter

should be on the same date each year. Let the children come up with reasons either to support or to argue against this view.

D Consider the crucial role of the sun in Easter celebrations and emphasise that without the sun there would be no life on earth. Many people all around the world observe the custom of watching the sunrise on Easter day, and many churches have Easter sunrise services. In olden days, some people even travelled to a prominent spot to see the sun dance, for it was believed that the sun would dance for joy on Easter day as a sign of great happiness because of the resurrection of Christ.

Children's writing about the significance of the sun in Easter celebrations could be combined with creative art and/or craft work. A useful sun template is provided on p. 85.

Activity 2: An Easter garden

Design and grow an Easter garden. You will need a large wooden or metal tray, some compost, a stone, an empty toilet roll tube, some pretty twigs, and an assortment of very small plants or flowers, together with three crosses made from wood or thick card. Fill the tray with compost, making a hill to represent Calvary at one end of the garden. Place the crosses on top of the hill. Position the empty toilet roll tube horizontally in the centre of the tray and cover it with compost, leaving one end exposed to represent the tomb of Jesus. Place the

stone to one side of the tomb entrance. Arrange twigs and small plants or tiny vases of flowers in the compost to decorate the garden. If you wish to be even more ambitious, plan your garden well ahead of time and sow grass seed to cover the hillside and garden surface. Spray the garden regularly with a mist sprayer to keep it fresh.

Make an Easter garden in the classroom

ART

Activity 1: Stained-glass window pictures
Design and make stained-glass window pictures, depicting scenes from the Easter story. Use **Copymaster 5** (Stained-glass window) as a starting point. This is an artist's interpretation of the crucifixion of Jesus and the two thieves, dated around 1900, which is in Norwich Cathedral. Discuss the content of the picture with the class before the children colour it to look like stained glass, then create further original designs. Use black paper or card for a background and cut openings in it, leaving a basic window framework. Place this over the picture, so that portions show through. Ideally the picture should be made from transparent materials such as coloured Cellophane® so that when it is displayed against a window the light will shine through.

Activity 2: Easter cards
Make Easter greeting cards. The scope is clearly enormous for variety of size, shape and design. Some suggestions are provided below, and the templates in Section 3 of this book will also be helpful. The suggested designs can be adapted to make models and three-dimensional collages.

[A] Cut a shape out of coloured card, as shown below, with 'doors' that fold over to hide the lower part of the creature inside. Write the words 'Happy Easter' on the outside of the doors, and colour them to look like wood. Stick a cut-out rabbit or chick on the inside, and decorate its surrounding edge with flowers or a message.

black card framework   openings cut out

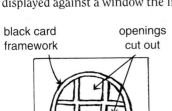

place framework over picture

open   closed

Encourage children to design their own folding Easter cards

B Make an egg card. Fold a rectangle of card in half, and cut out an oval shape with flattened base, leaving the fold intact. Cut a zig-zag line across the centre of the front of your oval as far as the hinge. Make a collage chick from yellow tissue paper or cotton wool, and place it on the uncut oval inside the card. Add pieces of felt for eyes and beak. Write an Easter message on the inside of the cut shape (i.e. inside the front half of the folded card).

Alternatively, make fluffy chick cards. Draw a chick in a happy Easter scene. Paint the background then pull out strands of cotton wool to glue on for the chick (yellow) and clouds (white). Glue on collage flowers.

C Design cards which contrast the blackness and gloom of Good Friday with happy and joyous symbols of Easter day. Paint black crosses on a hillside, and the surrounding landscape. Glue on collage symbols in the foreground such as daffodils, lilies, birds and butterflies.

Older pupils may like to make 'risen Christ' cards. Cut a doorway which opens in the front of a folded card. Colour the outside of this to look like a sealed tomb. Paint the risen Christ on the inside so that he is revealed when the 'tomb' is opened.

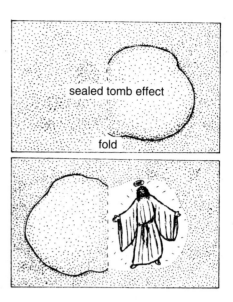

D Cut out a double thickness of card in the shape of a basket, using the template on p. 78. Fold this over, and decorate the front to resemble an Easter basket. Cut out egg shapes from pretty patterned wallpaper and glue these into the basket. Write the words 'Happy Easter' in the gap below the handle.

On a straightforward rectangular card, design an alternative Easter basket, as shown below (a template could be provided for the children to draw around). Attach collage flowers made out of tissue paper in a two-colour scheme.

E Make Easter bunny cards (see template on p. 81). Two possible designs are shown on page 9. Bunny and flowers can be painted or cut from paper, wallpaper or material to make a collage. The template on p. 81 gives the various parts needed to make up a collage bunny.

F Make Easter Swan cards. Again, a template for the swan is provided on p. 82. Cut out a card swan, then use white tissue paper to decorate the bird's body – layer pieces of tissue to create a feather effect. Pulled out cotton wool is ideal for the neck. Glue the swan to a rectangular card, taking care to insert a decorated egg shape behind the body before it is finally glued down.

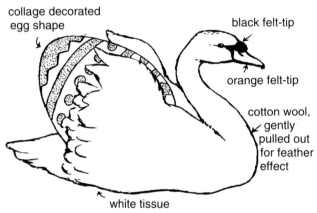

collage decorated
egg shape

black felt-tip

orange felt-tip

cotton wool,
gently
pulled out
for feather
effect

white tissue

A swan design for Easter

Activity 3: An Easter mélange

A Let the children make Easter bonnets. If they are able to bring in an old straw hat to decorate, then so much the better. If not, use any old hat, or for a very simple version, use a paper plate with two ribbons attached to tie under the chin. Decorate with anything you have available to make flowers, fruit, chicks and bunnies, perhaps utilising some of the templates and other art ideas in this topic. Wear your bonnets for an Easter assembly, or organise your own Easter parade in the neighbourhood or school grounds.

B Make Easter rabbit party invitations. These would be ideal if you are going to do some Easter cookery for a party in the classroom (for suitable recipes see pp. 92–3), or the children could take them home for their families to use. Draw the outline of half a rabbit on

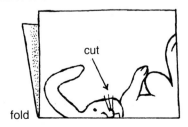

cut

fold

Have fun making and wearing Easter bonnets

to a piece of folded card. Cut out along the non-folded lines of the drawing, and colour it in. On the reverse, write the date, place and time of the party. This idea could, of course, be used for stand-up rabbit Easter cards.

C Younger children will enjoy colouring Easter egg patterns and designing their own. Use **Copymaster 6** (Egg patterns) for this purpose. Designs created could be used in other activities, such as decorating real blown egg-shells. Encourage pupils to incorporate a variety of Easter symbols in to their designs; they can cut out the eggs on the copymaster and use them as templates to generate more eggs. All material can then be collated into a colourful egg booklet.

D Make egg-shell rabbits. You will need to blow eggs (see p. 30) until they are empty (save insides for cooking). With a black felt-tip pen, mark a rabbit's face on the rounded end of each egg. Glue a cotton wool tail at the other end. Cut out ears from white felt and glue in place. Arrange them in a suitable place, such as in a small basket.

Egg-shell rabbits

E Decorate the inside of eggs. Blow an egg, then very carefully make a tiny hole with a needle on one long side of it. Using fine tweezers, chip away small pieces of shell until a substantial hole is revealed. Leave for a few hours so that any remaining moisture on the inside dries out. Glue whatever you wish inside the egg – perhaps a small rabbit or chick cut out of card, a felt butterfly, or a commercially bought chick (such as you can buy to decorate cakes). Mount the egg for display on a stand of Plasticine®.

Plasticine® stand

F Make Easter baskets. These could be made from any existing small basket, or from a cardboard box covered with yellow paper or pretty wallpaper. Fill the container with straw or crumpled green tissue paper. Decorate the outside in creative ways, using ribbon and paper flowers for a basket handle, and glued on lace, ribbon and collage flowers for a box. Fill the basket with decorated eggs, or use it for Easter biscuits (for recipe see p. 93).

G Make wool pompom chicks. Wind yellow wool around a circle of card with a hole in the centre. Keep winding until no more wool can go through the hole (use a needle when it gets tight). Cut around the edge of the circle, cutting through the loops of wool. Tie a piece of wool tightly around the centre. Remove lengths of wool and fluff them out into a pompom shape for the chick's head. Make a slightly larger pompom for its body. Secure the two together with glue. Finish your chick by gluing on feet, wings and a beak made from pieces of orange felt, and black felt eyes.

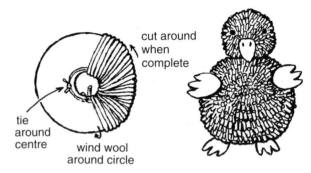

H Make an egg tree. Blow out a number of eggs and carefully thread fine cotton with a long needle through the holes you have made so that they can be hung. Decorate them as you wish. Hang from an interestingly shaped small branch or bendy willow twigs, secured in a vase or flower pot. If your twigs have no natural greenery, glue on leaves made from green paper or felt.

Decorate a classroom corner with an egg tree

A collection of decorated Easter baskets or boxes makes an eye-catching display

I Make 'egg hunt' pictures. Children should design and paint a picture of a garden, landscape or countryside scene, and conceal some eggs, carefully camouflaged in their work. They could then exchange pictures and hunt for each other's hidden eggs.

Activity 4: Easter in art
Introduce the children to well-known paintings which depict aspects of the Easter story by showing slides, consulting reference books on works of art or searching for reproduction pictures. Look, for example, for Rembrandt's *Descent from the Cross*, Gaugin's *Crucifixion*, Salvador Dali's *The Yellow Christ* and *The Last Supper* by Stanley Spencer. Many of the great Italian painters such as Piero della Francesca have also produced striking illustrations of the Easter story. Encourage pupils to discuss and explore aspects of Easter shown in paintings. Adapt a corridor or section of the classroom to create an Easter 'art gallery', displaying some of your pictures and accompanying written work.

RE

Activity 14: The Easter season
Make an illustrated diary or calendar of the Christian Easter season, with a page for each significant day, explaining its origins and importance. Days and periods to include are listed below (see the outline calendar in Section 3, p. 89).

Background information
● Ash Wednesday – This is the first day of Lent. The name derives from a custom which began in the days of Pope Gregory in the sixth century. He suggested that when someone was genuinely sorry for saying or doing something wrong, they should wear clothes made of sackcloth and should sprinkle ashes on their head.
● Palm Sunday – The day when Christians remember the triumphal entry of Jesus in Jerusalem at the beginning of the last week of his life. Jewish people tore down palm branches from the trees and waved them while shouting 'Hosannah!'
● Maundy Thursday – This is the Thursday before Good Friday, when a 'Royal Maundy' ceremony takes place and specially minted Maundy money is given away by the Queen (see p. 103 for further details).
● Good Friday – This is the Friday before Easter Sunday and is the day on which the Christian Church remembers the crucifixion of Christ at Golgotha. The word 'good' in this context means 'holy'. Hot-cross buns are eaten on this day as a reminder of Christ's cross (see p. 103).
● Easter Sunday – This is the day when Christians celebrate the resurrection of Jesus Christ from the dead.
● Holy Week – This is the term used to describe the period when Christians remember the last week of the life of Jesus, from Palm Sunday through to Easter Sunday.
● Lent – The period of 40 days which commences on Ash Wednesday and ends on Easter Sunday. It is a time when Christians remember how Jesus spent 40 days alone in the desert without food. He was tempted by Satan to disobey God, but Jesus resisted all temptations. Many people today mark the period of Lent by making sacrifices in their own lives, such as doing without certain foods (for example, meat, chocolate) which they particularly enjoy.

Activity 2: The first Easter
A Tell the Christian story of Easter, which is outlined in Section 2 of this book. In addition, with older children, read aloud or let pupils read the story as it is written in the Bible. Relevant verses from the Revised Standard Version of the Bible, with references, are detailed below.

Six days before the Passover, Jesus came to Bethany, where Lazarus was, whom Jesus had raised from the dead. There they made him a supper; Martha served, and Lazarus was one of those at table with him. Mary took a pound of costly ointment of pure nard and anointed the feet of Jesus and wiped his feet with her hair; and the house was filled with the fragrance of the ointment. But Judas Iscariot, one of his disciples (he who was to betray him), said, 'Why was this ointment not sold for three hundred denarii and given to the poor?' Jesus said, 'Let her alone. The her keep it for the day of my burial. The poor you always have with you, but you do not always have me.'
John 12:1–5, 7

The next day a great crowd who had come to the feast heard that Jesus was coming to Jerusalem. So they took branches of palm trees and went out to meet him, crying, 'Hosanna! Blessed is he who comes in the name of the Lord, even the King of Israel!' And Jesus found a young ass and sat upon it; as it is written, 'Fear not, daughter of Zion; behold, your king is coming, sitting on an ass's colt!' His disciples did not understand this at first; but when Jesus was glorified, then they remembered that this had been written of him and had been done to him.
John 12:12–16

Then came the day of Unleavened Bread, on which the passover lamb had to be sacrificed. And when the hour came, he sat at table, and the apostles with him. And he said to them, 'I have earnestly desired to eat this passover with you before I suffer; for I tell you I shall not eat it until it is fulfilled in the kingdom of God.' And he took a cup, and when he had given thanks he said, 'Take this, and divide it among yourselves; for I tell you that from now on I shall not drink of the fruit of the vine until the kingdom of God comes.' And he took bread, and when he had given thanks he broke it and gave it to them, saying, 'This is my body which is given for you. Do this in remembrance of me.' And likewise the cup after supper, saying, 'This cup which is poured out for you is the new covenant in my blood. But behold the hand of him who betrays me is with me on the table. For the son of man goes as it has been determined; but woe to that man by whom he is betrayed!'
Luke 22:7, 14–22

11

And they went to a place which was called Gethsemane; and he said to his disciples, 'Sit here, while I pray.' And he took with him Peter and James and John, and began to be greatly distressed and troubled. And he said to them, 'My soul is very sorrowful, even to death; remain here, and watch.' And going a little farther, he fell on the ground and prayed that, if it were possible, the hour might pass from him. And he said, 'Abba, Father, all things are possible to thee; remove this cup from me; yet not what I will, but what thou wilt.' And he came and found them sleeping, and he said to Peter, 'Simon, are you asleep? Could you not watch one hour? Watch and pray that you may not enter into temptation; the spirit indeed is willing, but the flesh is weak.' And again he went away and prayed, saying the same words. And again he came and found them sleeping, for their eyes were very heavy; and they did not know what to answer him. And he came the third time, and said to them, 'Are you still sleeping and taking your rest? It is enough; the hour has come; the Son of man is betrayed into the hands of sinners. Rise, let us be going; see, my betrayer is at hand.'

And immediately, while he was still speaking, Judas came, one of the twelve, and with him a crowd with swords and clubs, from the chief priests and the scribes and the elders. Now the betrayer had given them a sign, saying, 'The one I shall kiss is the man; seize him and lead him away under guard.' And when he came, he went up to him at once, and said, 'Master!' And he kissed him. And they laid hands on him and seized him. But one of those who stood by drew his sword, and struck the slave of the high priest and cut off his ear. And Jesus said to them, 'Have you come out as against a robber, with swords and clubs to capture me? Day after day I was with you in the temple teaching, and you did not seize me. But let the scriptures be fulfilled.' And they all forsook him, and fled.

Mark 14:32–50

Now at the feast the governor was accustomed to release for the crowd any one prisoner whom they wanted. And they had then a notorious prisoner, called Barabbas. So when they had gathered, Pilate said to them, 'Whom do you want me to release for you, Barabbas or Jesus who is called Christ?' For he knew that it was out of envy that they had delivered him up. Besides, while he was sitting on the judgment seat, his wife sent word to him, 'Have nothing to do with that righteous man, for I have suffered much over him today in a dream.' Now the chief priests and the elders persuaded the people to ask for Barabbas and destroy Jesus. The governor again said to them, 'Which of the two do you want me to release for you?' And they said, 'Barabbas.' Pilate said to them, 'Then what shall I do with Jesus who is called Christ?' They all said, 'Let him be crucified.' And he said, 'Why, what evil has he done?' But they shouted all the more, 'Let him be crucified.'

So when Pilate saw that he was gaining nothing, but rather that a riot was beginning, he took water and washed his hands before the crowd, saying, 'I am innocent of this man's blood; see to it yourselves.'

Matthew 27:15–24

And the soldiers led him away inside the palace (that is, the praetorium); and they called together the whole battalion. And they clothed him in a purple cloak, and plaiting a crown of thorns they put it on him. And they began to salute him, 'Hail, King of the Jews!' And they struck his head with a reed, and spat upon him, and they knelt down in homage to him. And when they had mocked him, they stripped him of the purple cloak, and put his own clothes on him. And they led him out to crucify him.

Mark 15:16–20

It was now about the sixth hour, and there was darkness over the whole land until the ninth hour, while the sun's light failed; and the curtain of the temple was torn in two. Then Jesus, crying with a loud voice, said, 'Father, into thy hands I commit my spirit!' And having said this he breathed his last. Now when the centurion saw what had taken place, he praised God, and said, 'Certainly this man was innocent!'

Luke 23:44–7

Then those who had seized Jesus led him to Caiaphas the high priest, where the scribes and the elders had gathered. Now the chief priests and the whole council sought false testimony against Jesus that they might put him to death, but they found none, though many false witnesses came forward. At last two came forward and said, 'This fellow said, "I am able to destroy the temple of God, and to build it in three days."' And the high priest stood up and said, 'Have you no answer to make? What is it that these men testify against you?' But Jesus was silent. And the high priest said to him, 'I adjure you by the living God, tell us if you are the Christ, the Son of God.' Jesus said to him, 'You have said so. But I tell you, hereafter you will see the Son of man seated at the right hand of Power, and coming on the clouds of heaven.' Then the high priest tore his robes, and said, 'He has uttered blasphemy. Why do we still need witnesses? You have now heard his blasphemy. What is your judgment?' They answered, 'He deserves death.'

Now Peter was sitting outside in the courtyard. And a maid came up to him, and said 'You also were with Jesus the Galilean.' But he denied it before them all, saying, 'I do not know what you mean.' And when he went out to the porch, another maid saw him, and she said to the bystanders, 'This man was with Jesus of Nazareth.' And again he denied it with an oath, 'I do not know the man.' After a little while the bystanders came up and said to Peter, 'Certainly you are also one of them, for your accent betrays you.' Then he began to invoke a curse on himself and to swear, 'I do not know the man.' And immediately the cock crowed. And Peter remembered the saying of Jesus, 'Before the cock crows, you will deny me three times.' And he went out and wept bitterly.

Matthew 26:57, 59–66, 69–75

When it was evening, there came a rich man from Arimathea, named Joseph, who also was a disciple of Jesus. He went to Pilate and asked for the body of Jesus. Then Pilate ordered it to be given to him. And Joseph took the body, and wrapped it in a clean linen shroud, and laid it in his own new tomb, which he had hewn in the rock; and he rolled a great stone to the door of the tomb, and departed.

Next day, that is, after the day of Preparation, the chief priests and the Pharisees gathered before Pilate and said, 'Sir, we remember how that impostor said, while he was still alive, "After three days I will rise again." Therefore order the sepulchre to be made secure until the third day, lest his disciples go and steal him away, and tell the people, "He has risen from the dead," and the last fraud will be worse than the first.' Pilate said to them, 'You have a guard of soldiers; go, make it as secure as you can.' So they went and made the sepulchre secure by sealing the stone and setting a guard.

Matthew 27:57–60, 62–6

Now on the first day of the week Mary Magdalene came to the tomb early, while it was still dark, and saw that the stone had been taken away from the tomb.

But Mary stood weeping outside the tomb, and as she wept she stooped to look into the tomb; and she saw two angels in white, sitting where the body of Jesus had lain, one at the head and one at the feet. They said to her, 'Woman, why are you weeping?' She said to them, 'Because they have taken away my Lord, and I do not know where they have laid him.' Saying this, she turned round and saw Jesus standing, but she did not know that it was Jesus. Jesus said to her, 'Woman, why are you weeping? Whom do you seek?' Supposing him to be the gardener, she said to him, 'Sir, if you have carried him away, tell me where you have laid him, and I will take him away.' Jesus said to her, 'Mary.' She turned and said to him in Hebrew, 'Rabboni!' (which means Teacher). Jesus said to her, 'Do not hold me, for I have not yet ascended to the Father; but go to my brethren and say to them, I am ascending to my Father and your Father, to my God and your God.' Mary Magdalene went and said to the disciples, 'I have seen the Lord'; and she told them that he had said these things to her.

On the evening of that day, the first day of the week, the doors being shut where the disciples were, for fear of the Jews, Jesus came and stood among them and said to them, 'Peace be with you.' When he had said this, he showed them his hands and his side. Then the disciples were glad when they saw the Lord.

John 20:1, 11–17

Eight days later, his disciples were again in the house, and Thomas was with them. The doors were shut, but Jesus came and stood among them, and said, 'Peace be with you.' Then he said to Thomas, 'Put your finger here, and see my hands; and put out your hand, and place it in my side; do not be faithless, but believing.' Thomas answered him, 'My Lord and my God!' Jesus said to him, 'Have you believed because you have seen me? Blessed are those who have not seen and yet believe.'

Now Thomas, one of the twelve, called the Twin, was not with them when Jesus came. So the other disciples told him, 'We have seen the Lord.' But he said to them, 'Unless I see in his hands the print of the nails, and place my finger in the mark of the nails, and place my hand in his side, I will not believe.'

John 20:19–20, 24–9

D Along similar lines, ask the children to design a newspaper of the present day, imagining that the Easter story is current news. They should have fun devising headlines and writing various articles for inclusion in it.

What would a New Testament newspaper have made of the Easter story?

B Older children can undertake a comparative study of the Gospel stories and research whether there are any variations in the story provided by the writers. In particular, they should investigate whether they all tell of the same sequence of events in the Garden of Gethsemane on Easter Sunday morning.

C Suggest that the children write their own 'news reports' of various aspects of the Easter story: for example, an account of Jesus' triumphant entry into Jerusalem, a report by a member of the crowd at the trial of Jesus, an 'eyewitness' account of the crucifixion, and a report of the Sunday morning's events written by one of the people involved. These could then be assembled, perhaps with the help of a computer, into a class newspaper telling of the whole story of Easter, with reports and accounts from the viewpoints of various people involved (including Mary, Pontius Pilate, Judas, the disciples).

Schools with access to desk top publishing facilities could produce extremely effective front pages, if not the entire newspaper. The children could inspect modern tabloid newspapers for appropriate features (advertisements, pictures, puzzles, crosswords, etc.) which could be adapted into entries for this biblical newspaper.

MUSIC

Activity 1: Easter in music

A A wealth of music, hymns and songs has been composed on aspects of the Easter story. Every school will no doubt possess a range of hymn and song books containing Easter music, both ancient and modern. In addition to teaching the children a range of hymns and songs to sing (*Lord of the Dance* is a fine example), listen to some well-known classical music that has been composed to celebrate the Easter festival.

Background information

A number of classical pieces of music have been written with an Easter theme. The most obvious, perhaps, is Handel's oratorio, *The Messiah*, with its famous 'Hallelujah Chorus'. Others include J.S. Bach's *Magnificat*, his *Mass in B Minor* and also his *St Matthew Passion*, together with Haydn's *Seven Last Words*, John Stainer's *Crucifixion*, Richard Wagner's 'Good Friday Spell' from Act 3 of '*Parsifal*', and Pietro Mascagni's 'Easter Hymn' from the opera *Cavalleria Rusticana*. For a more contemporary treatment of the Easter theme, why not try carefully selected extracts from the rock musicals *Godspell* and particularly *Jesus Christ Superstar*: songs such as 'Hosanna' and 'King Herod's Song' from the latter will appeal because of their melody and rhythm, and can be used to explain the attitudes of

people actually involved in the events of that first Easter week. On a lighter note, of course, is the perennial favourite 'Easter Bonnet' sung by Fred Astaire and Judy Garland on the film soundtrack recording of *Easter Parade*.

B When considering Easter music, listen to your chosen item(s) beforehand and, depending on the age and ability of the children, choose a passage or extract which you hope will appeal to them. Ask the children what the music signifies to them (bear in mind, it may not necessarily be 'Easter'!) and try to stimulate some creative writing or movement and dance based upon the music.

Background information

An excellent reference book when searching for appropriate pieces of music for topic work is *The Complete Book of Classical Music* by David Ewen, published by Robert Hale, London, originally in 1977. A similar book worthy of consultation with regard to the world of popular songs is *The Great Song Thesaurus* by Roger Lax and Frederick Smith, published by Oxford University Press in 1989. Both of these may be available in your local library.

Eostre

15

Palm Sunday

Fools! For I also had my hour;
One far fierce hour and sweet:
There was a shout about my ears,
And palms before my feet.

Easter word puzzle

2 across

5 across

1 down

1 across

3 down

2 down

3 across

4 across

Eastertime C3

Easter around the world

Draw a line to match each custom with its country.

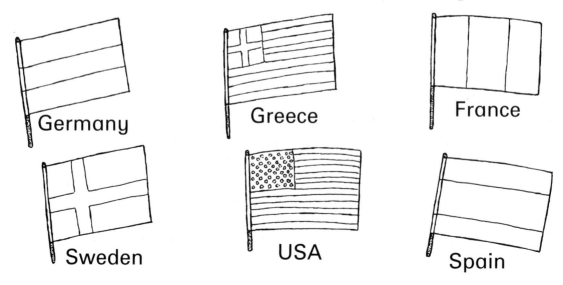

Germany

Greece

France

Sweden

USA

Spain

18

Stained-glass window

19

Egg patterns

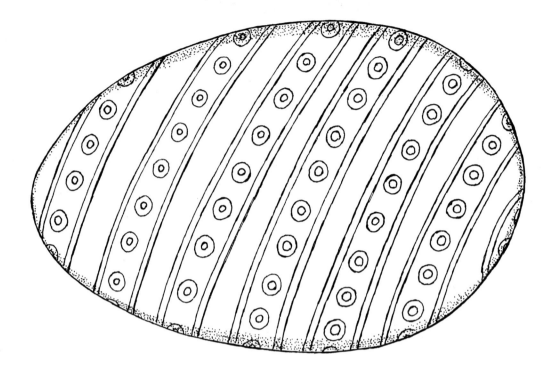

Colour the top egg, then design and colour your own pattern below.

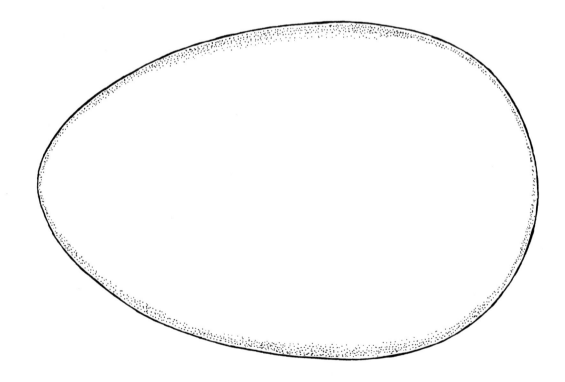

Eastertime C6

Eggs

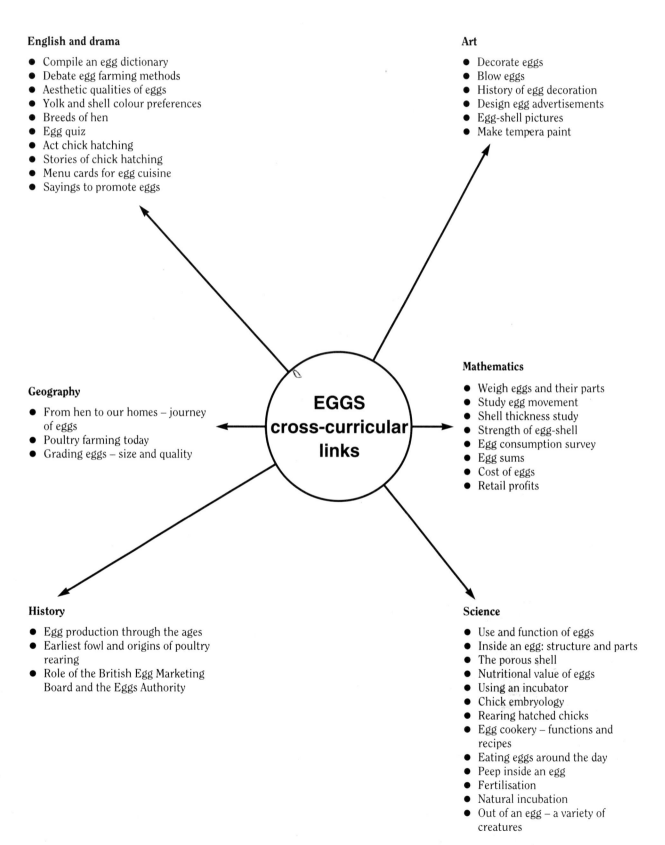

English and drama

- Compile an egg dictionary
- Debate egg farming methods
- Aesthetic qualities of eggs
- Yolk and shell colour preferences
- Breeds of hen
- Egg quiz
- Act chick hatching
- Stories of chick hatching
- Menu cards for egg cuisine
- Sayings to promote eggs

Art

- Decorate eggs
- Blow eggs
- History of egg decoration
- Design egg advertisements
- Egg-shell pictures
- Make tempera paint

Geography

- From hen to our homes – journey of eggs
- Poultry farming today
- Grading eggs – size and quality

EGGS cross-curricular links

Mathematics

- Weigh eggs and their parts
- Study egg movement
- Shell thickness study
- Strength of egg-shell
- Egg consumption survey
- Egg sums
- Cost of eggs
- Retail profits

History

- Egg production through the ages
- Earliest fowl and origins of poultry rearing
- Role of the British Egg Marketing Board and the Eggs Authority

Science

- Use and function of eggs
- Inside an egg: structure and parts
- The porous shell
- Nutritional value of eggs
- Using an incubator
- Chick embryology
- Rearing hatched chicks
- Egg cookery – functions and recipes
- Eating eggs around the day
- Peep inside an egg
- Fertilisation
- Natural incubation
- Out of an egg – a variety of creatures

SCIENCE

Activity 1: What is an egg?

A Consider this question, and ask the children to give their views on it – discuss the appearance, use and function of eggs in the world. Two key teaching points which should emerge are that all birds lay eggs, and that eggs form an important part of our diet. As part of this discussion, ask the children to consider whether we could live without eggs in the world. The answer is that bird life is entirely dependent on eggs for survival and continuation of the species.

B Carefully break open a hen's egg and closely observe its structure, preferably using magnifying equipment. Help the children to identify the various aspects of its structure. Use **Copymaster 1** (Inside an egg) to assist with this task. The sheet shows an enlarged egg, along with key parts of its structure. Ask pupils to colour the yolk in the centre, then to label the main features and undertake additional writing to explain them. (This could be linked with the compilation of a class 'egg dictionary' – see English activities). The following background material will help you to focus upon important aspects of the egg's structure.

Background information
- Rounded end and pointed end – Help the children to appreciate that an egg is not a perfect circle or oval. One end is more pointed than the other.
- Air space – At the rounded end of the egg is the air space, or air cell. Here the inner and outer membranes are separated by a bubble of air. When an egg is newly laid and very fresh, this air space is very small.
- Membranes – An egg has two membranes. The outer one is sometimes called the shell membrane. In the diagram on Copymaster 1, this is shown as being separate from the shell, but in an actual egg there is no space between the outer membrane and the shell. Close to this is the inner membrane, which encloses the white and yolk of the egg. Membranes act rather like thin filters of 'skin' and help to keep the egg in good condition.
- Shell – The hard exterior of the egg, which is porous (i.e. it has minute holes in it) serves three functions:
  (i) it prevents the inside of the egg from being damaged by minor bumps,
  (ii) it helps to keep the inside of the egg in good condition by slowing down the loss of water vapour from the inside into the air,
  (iii) it helps to prevent contamination of the inside of the egg by bacteria which could enter from the air.
- White – The correct name for this is albumen. When an egg is raw, the albumen is actually clear and only appears white when the egg is cooked.
- Yolk – The yellowy orange centre to the egg which is full of nutrients.
- Yolk membrane – Otherwise known as the vitelline

membrane, the thin shield which surrounds the yolk and holds it together. The children will appreciate that this is easily broken when an egg is cracked, but with care it can remain intact.
- Germinal disc – Seen as a tiny speck on the surface of the yolk. If an egg is fertilised, the embryo begins life in the disc.
- Chalazae – Appear as twisted, thickened strands within the white. They act as 'anchors' for the yolk, keeping it in place in the centre of the egg.

C Hard-boil an egg so that the children can see the air space more clearly. Shell the hard-boiled egg, and the space should be very apparent at the rounded end. Compare the size of the air space in a 'new' egg with one of similar size that has been stored for a few weeks.

Background information
Gradually, an egg loses water (in the form of vapour) from the inside through the membranes and shell into the air. As this happens, air is drawn through minute holes in the shell to replace the lost water. Thus the air space is slowly enlarged as the egg ages. The shell has more pores at the rounded end, which is why the air space can be seen here.

D Observe the pores in egg shells. You will need a piece of shell, preferably from the rounded end of an egg (since this has more pores than the pointed end), a piece of stiff card and a powerful torch or lamp. Cut a hole approximately 1 cm in diameter in the card, and glue or tape the shell over the hole. In a dark place, shine the torch through the hole and use a magnifying lens to observe the tiny specks of light coming through the shell: these are the pores which allow water vapour and air to be passed through the shell. When a chick embryo is growing inside, they enable the growing bird to obtain oxygen.

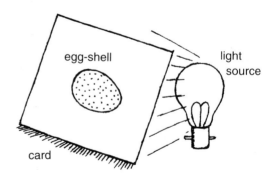

E Study the inside of an egg by making a hole in its shell and peering inside with the aid of a magnifying lens. Lie an egg on its side in a dish; using a pin, make a small hole in the shell on the upper surface, then use fine tweezers to remove a section of the shell. Continue to use the tweezers to remove the membranes from your window. Observe and sketch the magnified interior

– the chalazae should clearly be seen using this method of observation.

F Study the food value of eggs, using **Copymaster 2**, (The nutritious egg) as a starting point for this activity. The diagram on the copymaster shows the main components of an egg in their accurate proportions: these are water, fat (10.9 per cent), protein (12.3 per cent) and carbohydrate (0.4 per cent). Beneath the diagram are the key words which name the egg's components. Discuss the diagram and words with the children, noting that vitamins and minerals cannot be represented in the pie-chart as they are present in such tiny amounts. Children can colour the sections of the chart, then undertake further research about each of the components shown, and do accompanying writing to explain the importance of each. The key teaching point is that eggs are an extremely valuable source of nutrients and are thus very important in the diet of many people. Younger pupils who are unable to understand the mathematics of the pie-chart could perhaps write some sentences about why eggs are good for us, using the words shown on the copymaster.

Background information
A large part of an egg is made up of water. In addition, eggs contain five main nutrients needed and used by the human body.

● Protein – Important for growth. Egg protein is the highest quality protein there is. Around 12 per cent of the weight of the shell's contents is protein, which is found in both the white and the yolk, though the yolk of an egg contains a higher concentration of protein than its white.
● Fats – Give us energy (calories). Fats make up some 11 per cent of the weight of the shell's contents. Fats are a mixture of substances, including 'fatty acids' which may be 'saturated' or 'polyunsaturated'. Eggs have both types of fatty acids, though 63 per cent of the whole fat content of the egg is unsaturated.
● Carbohydrate – Main use in our body is to provide energy. An egg's carbohydrate content is very small – around 0.4 per cent (one part in 250) of the total weight of the egg.
● Vitamins – Eggs contain many vitamins which are essential for keeping our body healthy. The main function of vitamins is to enable the body to use its key nutrients (proteins, carbohydrates and fats) efficiently. Eggs contain Vitamin A, several vitamins in the B group, and Vitamins D and E. They do not contain Vitamin C. The vitamins assist our bodies in various ways. For example, Vitamin A helps to keep our skin and eyes healthy, Vitamin B12 helps to keep our blood in good condition, and Vitamin D helps keep our bones and teeth in good order.
● Minerals – Also help to keep our bodies in good condition, and they promote healthy growth. Two key minerals found in eggs are iron and calcium. Others include iodine, phosphorus, zinc and selenium.

Note The energy value of a size 3 egg is 80 calories.

G Organise a display based on the above information. Make a central collage figure alongside a picture of an egg containing a diagram from Copymaster 2. Surround these with writing about the significance of the various nutrients contained in eggs, and add two or three collage hens to remind children where most of the eggs that we eat derive from.

Activity 2: Incubating eggs
A Incubate some fertilised hens' eggs. This is a major project that should not be undertaken without a great deal of thought and preparation. Some background material is provided below, but teachers planning to undertake this project are strongly urged to do further reading on the subject: *An Incubator in the Classroom* by A. Trotman and J. Palmer (1986), is a useful and inexpensive practical guide published by NAEE Publications, Wolverhampton Polytechnic, The Gorway, Walsall, Staffs WS1 3BD. When planned and executed with care and attention to detail, the activity of incubating eggs can be enormously rewarding and successful, helping children to learn elements of embryology, the necessity for fertilisation if an egg is to develop into a chick, and providing them with the great excitement of being able to observe new life hatching from the eggs at the appropriate time.

Background information
Some essential questions should be considered before engaging in this activity. These include:

● Do I have a source of fertile eggs? So many schools are disappointed when nothing hatches: often the incubator is blamed when the actual cause is infertility of the eggs.
● Do I have suitable incubation equipment and the time which is necessary? An observation incubator (a purpose-made piece of electrical equipment which allows children to see through its covering and watch the eggs inside) is essential. Two makes of observation incubator are recommended, one available from Curfew Incubators of Buttons Hill, Southminster Road, Aithorne, Essex CH3 6EN, and the other from Philip Harris Ltd, Lynn Lane, Shenstone, Lichfield, Staffs WS14 0EE. Some Local Authorities have incubators

which can be loaned out to schools, but a far more satisfactory arrangement is for a school or group of schools to buy one. The incubator must be equipped with a wet and dry bulb thermometer as supplied by the firm for their incubator. Other equipment you will need includes a plastic mist sprayer, as the eggs have to be kept moist during the incubation period; a brood lamp with a red glass infra-red bulb to keep the young birds warm when they have hatched; a cardboard or wooden enclosure with sides at least 30 cm high for your 'brood' compartment; and suitable water fountains and food troughs.

● Do I have a supply of suitable food ready for the hatched birds? Finely chopped hard-boiled or scrambled egg or crumbed digestive biscuit dampened with milk can be given on the day of hatching and 'No 1 Chick Crumbs' after that. Young chicks drink continually, and fresh, clean water must always be available.

● Am I prepared to devote weekends and possibly holiday periods to the care of the eggs and young birds?

● Do I have a good permanent home for the young birds, who obviously cannot live in the classroom for ever (usually they can stay happily there for three to four weeks after hatching).

If the answer to all of these questions is yes, then do go ahead with this exciting activity. Other key points to consider and conduct further research upon include the following.

● Setting up the incubator correctly, paying due attention to ventilation, humidity and temperature. The thermometer usually has an incubation zone marked on it, which is 38–41°C (101–105°F): 39°C (103°F) is the mean for ordinary hens. Other species do vary, so check this point if you are incubating eggs of other birds such as ducks, pheasants or geese.

● Checking the length of the incubation period in days. Hens' eggs take 21 days to develop, while ducks' take 28 to 32 days according to breed, pheasants' 22 to 27 days and geese 28 to 30 days. Plan your schedule so that the eggs are due to hatch on a school day: avoid Fridays, Saturdays and Sundays, for obvious reasons.

● Ensuring that your eggs are fertile. Stipulate this on an order from a farm or supplier.

● Marking the eggs on one side with a pencil cross before placing them in the incubator. This is because they must be turned over regularly, and the mark enables children to check that all eggs have been turned. The eggs should be turned twice daily until four days before hatching is due. This must include weekends and half-term holidays. The interval between turning should be as long as possible (i.e. first thing upon arrival at school and last thing before leaving in the evening) so that the night-time period is not excessively longer than the daytime. The purpose of turning is to help the eggs to warm evenly and prevent the membranes from sticking to the inside of the shell. Children should warm their hands before turning the eggs. Eggs should always be turned by rolling them gently along the long axis, not by somersaulting them end to end. Stop turning on the eighteenth day.

● Retaining constant humidity by spraying the eggs each day with warm water (around 37–39°C). Just before hatching, raise humidity by spraying two to three times a day.

● Discovering more about hatching and brooding. Chicks should remain in the incubator for up to 24 hours after hatching, until they are dry and fluffy. They often sleep for long periods during this time, so do not wake them to see if they are alive. Chicks need neither food nor water for the first 24 hours after hatching. Thereafter, they must be kept at the correct temperature in a brooding box and given constant supplies of food and fresh water. Temperatures to aim for inside this box are as follows:

first week: 32°C (90°F)
second week: 27°C (80°F)
third week: 21°C (70°F)
fourth week: 16°C (60°F).

[C] Clearly, the above activity provides tremendous scope for scientific tasks and understanding, both when the eggs are in the incubator and during the brooding period. Embryology is the first key topic for study. Use **Copymaster 3** (Growth of a chick in its egg), as a starting point in helping children to appreciate the stages of growth of the embryo during the incubation period. Pupils should enjoy colouring each of the diagrams and discussing the stages of development depicted. Perhaps enlarged versions of these diagrams could be made to build up an embryology display on the classroom wall.

[D] Study the development and growth of the chicks, once hatched. Suitable tasks and/or observations include:

● weighing the growing birds on a daily basis (taking care not to handle them any more than is absolutely necessary) and making graphs to show their steady gain in weight. Chicks can be weighed by placing them carefully in a small bag and suspending from a spring balance;

● structure and colouration;

● the development of feathers;

● studies of behaviour including movement, preening, feeding and drinking patterns, relationships between chicks in a group, instinct to cluster, circumstances in which the voice is used, and patterns of sleeping and activity.

With young children, studies of the above suggestions will come through incidental rather than directed observation, but may stimulate a great deal of discussion leading to creative writing and drawing rather than formal ways of recording. Older children should be encouraged to plan and carry out more formal investigations and testing of hypotheses, with appropriately designed recording mechanisms.

Activity 3: Eggs to eat

A Make a study of egg cookery, and put some recipes to the test. Begin by asking the children to name ways in which eggs can be cooked – for example, boiled, poached, fried, baked, scrambled – and then to suggest some common ways in which they are eaten, such as scrambled egg on toast, in an omelette, or fried with other foods. Go beyond these obvious dishes to investigate foods in which eggs are 'hidden' ingredients, such as cakes, custards, some sauces, pancakes and mayonnaise. This could be done either by providing some specialist cookery books or by asking the children to read through some general recipe books and identify items containing eggs as an ingredient.

B Follow on from the above activity by making an 'Eggs around the day' frieze, showing that eggs can be eaten in a wide variety of ways, and at all meals of the day. Individual pupils could make paintings of foods containing eggs to represent various times of the day. Cut these out, using a large egg-shaped template, and display around a central 'egg' which could simply be decorated or could contain egg cookery words.

C Cook some dishes requiring eggs, to demonstrate the various methods of preparing them. At a basic level, let the children fry eggs, noting the change in the colour of the albumen and in the texture of the whole egg as it cooks; make a simple omelette; boil some eggs, perhaps to demonstrate the difference between hard and soft boiled; and scramble some eggs. Ask the children to discuss differences in the taste of eggs cooked in these various ways. Make a graph to show children's preferences, and see which form of cooking is the class favourite.

D Undertake some more challenging egg cookery, using one or more of the recipes provided on pages 92–3. Ask the children to discuss egg cookery with their parents, and bring to school any other favourite 'tried and tested' recipes. Compile a class egg cookery book. If this can be typed or word-processed and suitably illustrated by older pupils, it could be offered for sale as a small business venture, leading to extensive related work in mathematics (costing, income, calculating profit, etc.).

Note Great care for the children's safety should always be taken when they are engaged in cookery activities. They should be supervised closely at all times when dealing with heat sources, hot ingredients and sharp implements.

'Eggs around the day' frieze

E With older children, discuss some of the reasons why eggs are important in cookery, apart from their flavour and nutritional value. Children may be able to appreciate how eggs react under different circumstances, enabling various dishes to be made.

Background information
Eggs play a key role in cookery processes. They are capable of *foaming* (i.e. incorporating air when beaten to help make soufflés, meringues, cakes and mousses), *coagulating* (i.e. binding other ingredients together or sealing foods) and *emulsifying* or acting as a base for sauces.

Activity 4: Eggs and fertilisation

A Emphasise the fact that in order for a young creature to develop inside an egg, fertilisation is necessary, requiring both a male and a female adult.

Explain to the children that most of the eggs we purchase and eat have not been fertilised and need not be. Even if they are, they have not begun to develop because they have not been incubated. (This should allay the fears of those who as a result of this topic may worry that they are boiling or scrambling a young bird!) Depending on the age of the children, you can obviously go into greater detail about the differences between hens and cockerels, and about the mating process. (Templates on pp. 76 and 77 may be useful for this activity.)

B Following on from the above discussion, help the children to recognise that the natural method of incubation does not involve electrical equipment. Talk about, and, if possible, find pictures of, a 'broody hen' incubating her eggs naturally.

● Use **Copymaster 4** (Out of an egg) to help the children appreciate that poultry (and other birds) are not the only creatures which hatch their young from eggs. It should be emphasised here that this topic focuses mainly on hens' eggs and related activities. This is because of the theme of the book as a whole, and the fact that chicks are usually the birds associated with Eastertime. Nevertheless, the topic would not be complete without reminding pupils that while *all* birds develop in eggs, some members of other animal families (i.e. mammals, reptiles, amphibians and fish) also hatch from eggs. A key teaching point is to help the children to appreciate that often we think of the term 'egg' as referring to an object with a hard shell and inner yolk and white. The word is often used, however, to describe embryonic forms without a shell, as, for example, in the case of frogs and toads. Suggest that the children identify the creatures depicted on the copymaster, colour them accurately, then use reference material to find out about their eggs and reproductive habits.

Background information
Creatures shown are:

1. Sea Turtle	5. Penguin
2. Spiny anteater	6. Platypus
3. Crocodile	7. Toad
4. Cobra	8. Robin

A key matter for investigation is which of these are birds. The robin has been included as a reminder that 'everyday' birds hatch from eggs in the same way as hens' chicks. Many of the other creatures are far more exotic and unusual. Explain to the children that amphibians, reptiles and fish commonly lay eggs, but with mammals (the platypus), this is an oddity.

GEOGRAPHY

Activity 1: Egg production

A Pursue a topic on egg production. This could include two substantial dimensions: (i) journey from the hen to our homes; (ii) farming techniques.

In the first instance, trace the journey of an egg from the hen to the consumer. A wall frieze can be made showing the various stages involved, each of which could be explored in greater detail with the aid of specialist reference books on chickens and egg production.

B Find out more about testing and grading eggs. If possible, take the children to a supermarket to see a range of eggs on display, all suitably boxed and labelled; or take a variety of sizes (with their boxes) into the classroom for observation.

Background information
Every egg sold in the UK (apart from those sold actually on a farm) is bound by regulations of the European

eggs are collected → they are checked and graded → they are carefully packed → SIZE 3 → they are despatched to stores → EGG CO. → we purchase them → they are stored in our homes until we are ready to eat them

Community which are designed to ensure quality and size, and to provide adequate information for the consumer. Grading of quality may be Class A (clean, fresh, perfect eggs; shells intact, small air spaces), Class B (have had to be cleaned or preserved; perhaps cracked or enlarged air spaces) or Class C (which could be used for some manufacturing processes, but cannot be sold to the public). Eggs are also size graded, in bands 1 to 7:

Size 1 70 g or over in weight
Size 2 65 g and under 70 g
Size 3 60 g and under 65 g
Size 4 55 g and under 60 g
Size 5 50 g and under 55 g
Size 6 45 g and under 50 g
Size 7 under 45 g.

C Use **Copymaster 5** (Egg box) as a basis for discussion of quality and grading. Ask each child to bring an empty egg box from home and faithfully to record what is on it on the enlarged box on the copymaster. They should write or illustrate six pieces of information on the copymaster – quantity of eggs in box, size designation, grade of quality, packing period/sell by date, name and address of the grader and the registered number. This activity will help them to appreciate that all packing stations in the UK have a number. All UK stations have a number beginning with a 9, followed by a regional number, then a specific station identification number. Display a range of completed copymasters, so that information can be compared. If possible, arrange a visit to a local packing factory to supplement your classroom work.

D Use specialist books on chicken farming to find out about methods of poultry rearing on farms. Find out about and discuss the differences between free-range farming, deep-litter methods and battery housing. Older children should be able to discuss the advantages and disadvantages of each method (relate this work to **English and drama** activities).

Egg production then and now

HISTORY

Activity 1: Egg production through the ages

A Investigate how egg production has changed over the years and examine reasons for this change. Key factors to consider include changes in lifestyles (there are now many more city dwellers), changes in transport (eggs can now be transported in a short time over long distances), technological developments (such as refrigeration, technology associated with battery farming), and developments in diet and food technology.

B Consolidate the above by designing and making a pair of parallel wall displays on 'then and now' of egg production, one showing a typical farmyard scene of some 200 years ago and the other depicting life on a modern poultry farm (link this work with **Geography** activities).

C Find out more about the very early history of egg consumption. Explain that the ancestors of modern fowls lived in the hot jungles of Asia. They laid their eggs in wild nests, like most birds of the present day. Gradually, people discovered how good these eggs were to eat, and designed simple cages in which to keep such fowl. By Roman times, the idea of keeping hens for egg production and consumption had become established in Britain. In the early days of farming, however, this was very much a secondary activity. Only in recent years has battery egg production become 'big business' and a sole method of farming for many people. The British Egg Marketing Board was established in 1957, and anyone who owned more than 50 hens had to register with the Board. In 1971, this Board was replaced by the Eggs Authority, a marketing organisation whose work includes advertising and sales promotion, public relations and information work and market research.

D Try to find pictures of the 'little lion' symbol of the British Egg Marketing Board. This emblem used to be printed on each egg, together with its weight grade of the times – large, standard, medium or small.

ENGLISH AND DRAMA

Activity 1: An egg dictionary

A Compile an 'egg dictionary'. As the whole topic progresses, suggest that the children enter each new 'egg word' they come across, together with a definition and an appropriate illustration. This could be done as a class exercise so that the dictionary can be displayed as a work of reference to be consulted and added to. As well as helping children to understand the meaning of egg-related words, this activity also gives practice in the task of putting words in their correct alphabetical order.

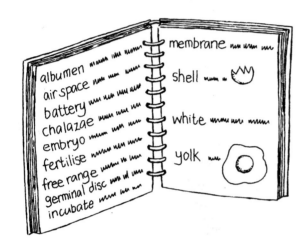

An egg dictionary

B Organise a class debate on the advantages and disadvantages of various methods of poultry farming. Some could argue strongly that battery farming is cruel and should be banned, while others can dispute this view, giving good reasons for their argument (link this work with **Geography** activities).

C Talk about the aesthetic qualities of eggs and make a list of words to describe their colour and shape: for example, smooth, round, shiny, speckled. Ask the children whether they have a preference for brown eggs or white eggs, and to say why: is it purely a matter of appearance, or do they think that there is a difference in taste? Discuss also the fact that some yolks are darker than others. Conduct a survey to find out what colour shells and yolks children in the class or school prefer. Let the pupils suggest how this survey might be carried out and how the results will be recorded.

Background information
Yolk and shell colour depends on the breed of the hen producing the egg. Generally, the darker the feathers of the hen, the darker will be her egg; lighter breeds lay 'white' eggs. The nutritional value is the same, irrespective of shell colour.

D The above activity could well link with a more scientific investigation into breeds of hens. Preferably, visit a farm with a variety of breeds, or use reference material to assist your enquiries. Identify and illustrate any breeds observed. Display pictures of them alongside accurately coloured pictures of their eggs.

E Use **Copymaster 6** (Egg quiz) as an aid to consolidating much of the information that has been introduced in the topic. Children can solve this individually with the help of appropriate reminders and reference books, or they can test each other in pairs.

Background information
Correct answers to Copymaster 6 are:

1. Air space
2. Yolk
3. Calazoe
4. Calcium, iron
5. Vitamin C
6. Germinal disc.
7. (a) 21; (b) 28–32
8. 1971
9. Free range, deep litter, battery
10. They all need eggs to make them

F Discuss what happens when a chick hatches from its egg, especially if the children have not had the opportunity to observe incubation at first hand. Consider what this is like for the chick –what will its movements be like, its expression, its feelings? In a drama lesson, let the children act out this process. They should begin by lying curled up tightly in a space on the floor, and end by standing and walking, uncertainly, as a representation of the chick using its legs for the first time.

G Write imaginative stories about chicks hatching from eggs. For example, ask the children to imagine they are a young bird hatching out, and to describe their feelings – of anticipation, wonder, excitement, determination, exhaustion – on entering the world.

H Design and write menu cards for an imaginary restaurant which specialises in egg cuisine. Think up a good name for the restaurant!

I Tell the children of some well-known sayings that have been used to promote the sale of eggs over the years: for example, 'Happiness is egg-shaped', 'Fresh from the nest – only the best will be stamped with the lion', 'Go to work on an egg', 'Get cracking'. Discuss their meanings and messages. Find out what slogans are used to advertise eggs today (link this work with art activities).

J Invite children to research, write about and role-play creation stories and myths involving eggs. Encourage them to invent their own.

MATHEMATICS AND TECHNOLOGY

Activity 1: Weighing an egg
A Weigh eggs of various Class sizes. Test, for example, to see whether a sample of Size 1 eggs all weigh the same (and correct) amount.

B Calculate the weight of various separated parts of an egg. Weigh the whole thing, then carefully crack it, remove the shell, then separate the yolk from the white. See which of the three components is heaviest, and which is lightest. Does the sum of the three components add up to the weight of the whole uncracked egg?

Activity 2: How does an egg move?
A Make a study of egg movement. Place an egg on a flat surface. Blow it gently and watch it roll. Before commencing this, ask the children to predict how the egg will move (i.e. do they think it will go in a straight line?) Test the predictions with as large a sample of eggs as possible.

Background information
The egg will move in a curved path, as it rolls almost in a circle, back to where it started. Discuss why this is so (this is clearly related to the shape of the egg's surface).

B Test a fascinating difference in the movement of cooked and uncooked eggs. Spin a cooked egg, quickly stop it with a finger and release it . . . it will stay still. Repeat with an uncooked egg. Children should be interested to see that this carries on spinning.

C Older children can invent and construct egg vehicles propelled by the movement (rolling, swinging, etc.) of one or more eggs. Test and race vehicles to find the most successful.

Activity 3: How thick is an egg-shell?
A Attempt to measure the thickness of an egg-shell. Study a piece of shell broken from an egg alongside a ruler. Let the children suggest whether the shell's thickness is the same as, greater than or less than one millimetre. If the answer is less than, ask them to estimate how many thicknesses of shell would be required to make a depth of a millimetre. Try to achieve this using more fragments of shell. If a micrometer is available, use this special apparatus to measure the precise thickness of shell.

B Discuss the merits of thick and thin shells. What are the advantages and disadvantages for the egg and for the embryonic bird inside?

Activity 4: How strong is an egg?
Ask older children to devise experiments to determine what weight (mass) is needed to crush an egg. One suitable set of apparatus is shown opposite. Consider whether an egg is actually very delicate or very strong. The pupils may be surprised at how much load a shell can take before breaking.

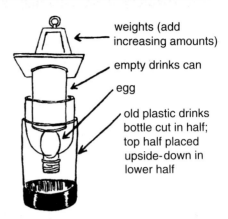
weights (add increasing amounts)
empty drinks can
egg
old plastic drinks bottle cut in half; top half placed upside-down in lower half

Egg-crushing apparatus

Activity 5: An egg survey
A Conduct a survey to find out approximately how many eggs are consumed in an 'average' week by each child, each child's family, and by the class as a whole (with or without families). Before doing this, decide whether you will just count eggs eaten as such (boiled, scrambled, poached, on toast, etc.) or whether you will attempt to calculate hidden egg consumption (in cakes, savoury dishes, etc.) by asking parents how many eggs they buy each week. Graph the results in a suitable way. This activity will lead to an investigation of egg 'statistics': for example, hens in the UK lay some 13 000 million eggs per year.

B Discuss the fact that eggs are usually sold in dozens or half dozens. Design egg sums for the children to solve, for example:

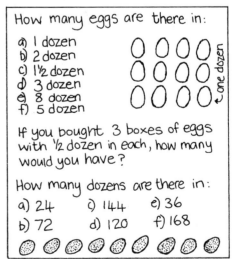
How many eggs are there in:
a) 1 dozen
b) 2 dozen
c) 1½ dozen
d) 3 dozen
e) 8 dozen
f) 5 dozen
If you bought 3 boxes of eggs with ½ dozen in each, how many would you have?
How many dozens are there in:
a) 24   c) 144   e) 36
b) 72   d) 120   f) 168

C Extend the above activity by linking calculations to costs. Research the current cost of a dozen eggs of various grades and sizes, and design shopping calculations for the children to solve.

D If you have a co-operative local shopkeeper, ask how many eggs are sold in an average day, week or year. If he or she is prepared to discuss prices, then retail profits could be calculated.

ART

Activity 1: Decorate eggs

A In order to decorate eggs, the children will need to learn how to 'blow' eggs gently to remove the yolk and white. This requires patience. Make two tiny holes, one in the rounded end of the egg and the other in the more pointed end, by carefully inserting a large sewing needle. Hold the egg over a dish, then blow through one hole, allowing the liquid gradually to drip out of the other.

Blowing an egg

B Blown eggs can be decorated in many ways. Patterns can be made on their shells with paint or felt-tip pens, which can then be varnished. A variety of materials such as felt, card, string, sequins, straw, tissue paper, coloured pipe cleaners, and so on, can be glued to the surface of an egg to create collage effects. Indeed, egg 'characters' may represent people, birds or animals (a range of possible designs is shown on page 75), but inevitably the children will enjoy creating their own original decorated eggs. The egg templates on page 74 will be useful for practising and developing designs before they are transferred on to the surface of real eggs. This sheet could also be used simply for making up patterns and designs to be coloured for a two-dimensional display.

Note Warn children that decorated hard-boiled eggs should never be eaten as they may contain toxins from the decoration.

C Remind the children that for thousands of years, people around the world have decorated eggs. Consult further reference material to find pictures of eggs that have been decorated for ornamental purposes. Perhaps some of these designs could be copied by the children.

Activity 2: Eggs in art

A Look for egg advertisements from various sources. Study them carefully to see what messages and images they portray. Ask the children to imagine that they are employed by the Eggs Authority, and have to design and illustrate advertisements that will encourage the public to buy more eggs.

B Make egg-shell pictures. This is a very useful way of using up shells of eggs left behind after classroom cooking or other investigations. Note that card is a better base than paper, as egg-shell is relatively heavy and needs firm glue to stick it down. Children will no doubt enjoy designing their own 'mosaic' pictures, though an obvious starting point is to make a picture of a large egg cracking open with a collage chick coming out of it!

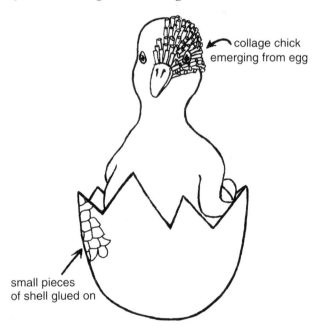

collage chick emerging from egg

small pieces of shell glued on

C Make tempera paint. This is simply egg white, slowly and thoroughly mixed with powder paint. Add the latter a little at a time. This creates a thick paste that can obviously be made in a variety of colours and used as paint. The use of tempera paint dates from the Middle Ages: use reference books to study some paintings that have been created using this medium. Ask children about its texture and use this as an opportunity to explore the differences between tempera, oil, watercolour, acrylic and other painting mediums.

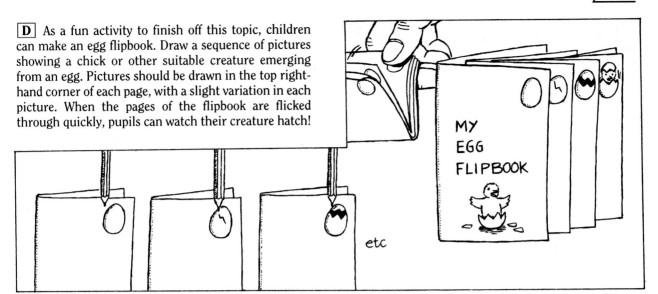

D As a fun activity to finish off this topic, children can make an egg flipbook. Draw a sequence of pictures showing a chick or other suitable creature emerging from an egg. Pictures should be drawn in the top right-hand corner of each page, with a slight variation in each picture. When the pages of the flipbook are flicked through quickly, pupils can watch their creature hatch!

etc

MY
EGG
FLIPBOOK

Inside an egg

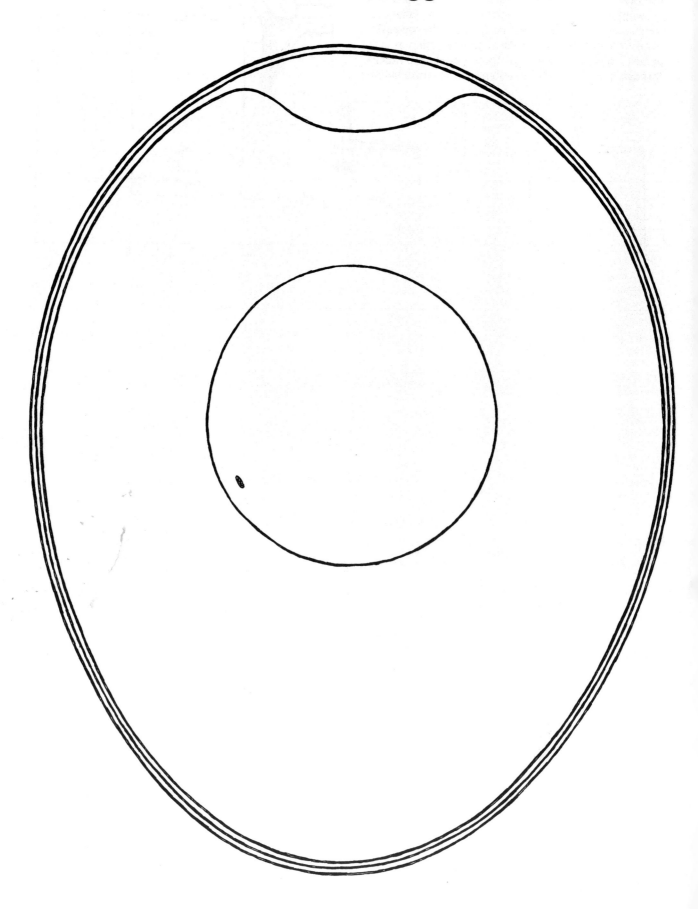

Eggs C1

The nutritious egg

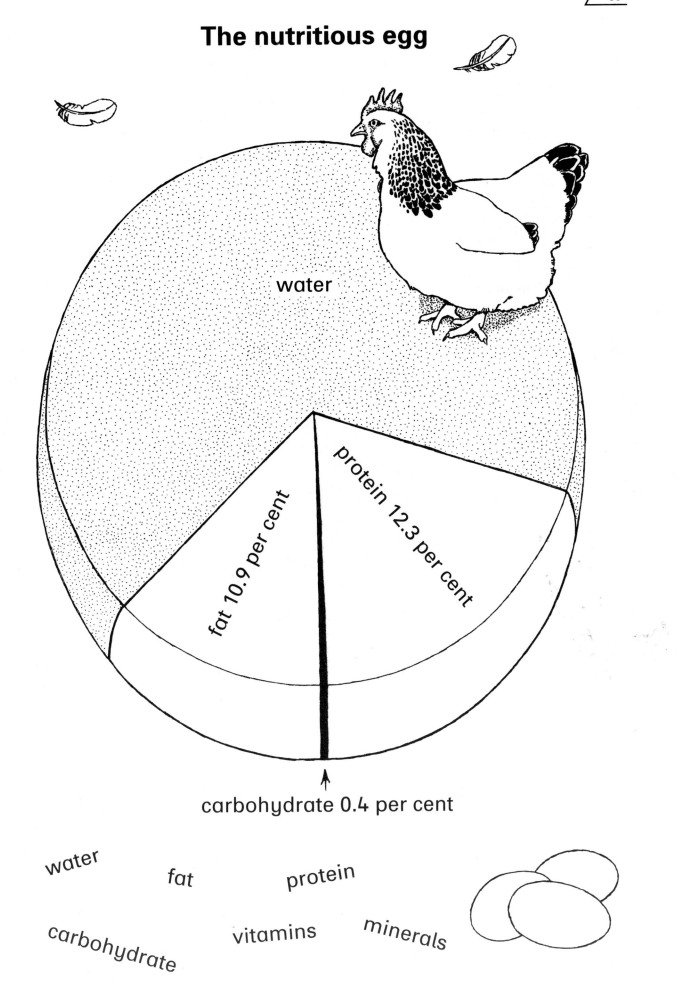

water

fat 10.9 per cent

protein 12.3 per cent

↑
carbohydrate 0.4 per cent

water   fat   protein

carbohydrate   vitamins   minerals

Growth of a chick in its egg

day 7	day	day
day	day 15	day
day	day	day 21

Out of an egg

Egg box

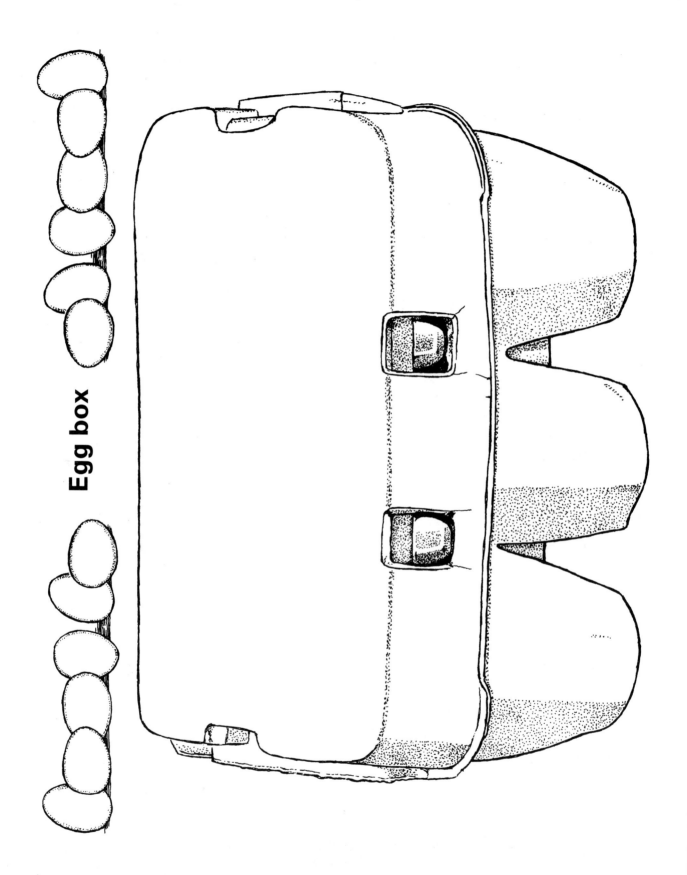

Egg quiz

1. Which part of the egg gets larger as the egg gets older?

2. Which part of the egg has most protein in it?

3. What holds the yolk suspended in the albumen?

4. Name the two main minerals found in eggs.

5. Which major vitamin is not found in eggs?

6. If an egg is fertilised, where does the chick begin to develop in the egg?

7. How many days does it take for (a) hen's and (b) duck eggs to develop in the egg before hatching?

8. When was the British Eggs Authority established?

9. Name three methods of rearing poultry used today.

10. What do the following foods have in common: omelette, mousse, fairy cake, piperade, soufflé?

Eggs C6

Life cycles

English and RE

- Ideas about 'beginnings'
- Events which mark beginnings
- Beginnings, change and endings
- The inevitability of change
- Creation of the world
- Things that do and do not change
- 'Dramatic change' stories
- People who change the world
- Changes in our everyday lives
- Ideas about loyalty and betrayal
- Make a life cycles dictionary/card index
- Gifts of newness
- Themes of repentance and renewal

Art and technology

- Collage butterfly pictures
- Three-dimensional butterflies for display
- Life cycle needlecraft collages
- Frog spawn pictures
- Croaking frog collages
- Paint and print caterpillars

LIFE CYCLES cross-curricular links

Music and drama

- Story of an imaginary lifetime
- 'Portrait of a life' operatic show

Science

- Study butterfly and moth life cycles
- Rear caterpillars
- Parts of a plant
- Parts of a seed
- Grow some seeds
- Life cycle of a flowering plant
- Conditions necessary for plant growth
- Pollination
- Life cycle of a frog
- Field investigations – animal and plant life cycles
- Human reproduction
- Inheritance of characteristics
- Gestation periods
- Concept of evolution
- Life cycle 'snap' card game

ENGLISH AND RE ▶

Activity 1: Easter 'beginnings'

A Discuss and write about the idea of 'beginnings'. Ask the children to name some well-known days or events that mark some of life's beginnings – the first day of a new year or term at school, a birthday which marks the beginning of a new year of our life, the birth of a baby, a wedding, the first day in a new job, the day a new discovery is made, the day which marks the accession to power of a new leader such as sovereign or a prime minister, etc.

An alternative approach would be to provide the children with a list of events and work out what they have in common: for example, people getting married, babies being born, new discoveries being made, sunrise, seeds being sown, new books being written and read for the first time. The answer of course is that all of these events are new, fresh or at the beginning of their life phase.

B Encourage pupils to collect family photographs and magazine cuttings to incorporate into a wall frieze called 'Beginnings', along with children's illustrations of happenings such as those listed above and others they can think of, accompanied by writing about how each may change and develop as time goes by. This activity should help to develop children's understanding and appreciation of the concept of 'change', and the fact that many things in the world (both living and non-living) have beginnings, life cycles, changes and, indeed, endings.

C Discuss and role-play emotions involved in the beginnings of various events. Children can act out sketches to show, for example, the happiness of parents at the birth of a baby, the 'Eureka!' experience of a scientist who has just made a new discovery, someone awaking with excitement at the start of a new day, an author who has just completed a new book which he or she hopes will be a bestseller, a chick struggling to get out of its egg, and so on. These and other examples could also be subjects for creative writing and the composition of poetry.

D Develop the above activity by discussing the extent to which we, as human beings, have power to influence the development of things/events/lives after their beginnings. The depth to which this can be explored will obviously depend on the age and ability of the children. At a simple level, aim to help children to appreciate that many things inevitably change during their lives (link to science activities: tadpoles to frogs, caterpillars to moths, seeds to plants, babies to adults, etc.) and this is part of the natural world. There is nothing we can do as humans to delay or stop certain changes in the world around us. With older children, this provides an excellent link into aspects of moral and environmental education – for example, the fact that people engage in various practices such as deforestation and hunting which alter the natural balance and cycle of life and death in the world.

A 'beginnings' wall frieze

Activity 2: New beginnings – the creation of the world

These ideas could be linked through RE at Eastertime to the Christian story of the creation of the world. Consider the following statement:

> Although the earth and all that we mean by 'the world' was created by God for us to enjoy, people have not always made the best of what has been entrusted to us. We only have to look around us to see that people have changed the world, and not always for the better.

Debate this statement, asking the children's views on whether they agree with it or not, and if so, why. Perhaps they could consider the answer to the following: if Jesus came back into the world today, what would he like least about it? What would he be pleased about?

Activity 3: Comings and goings with the passage of time

[A] Living things all have their lifetimes: they come and go, empires rise and fall, fashions change. Consider what leaves the world from time to time, and what endures through time. In the first instance, make lists of things in these two categories; then more elaborate writing or displays can be produced by the class.

WE COME AND GO:
← dodo
individual creatures
fashions
architectural styles
rulers and governments
food preferences
many buildings
many forms of art
and music
platform → shoes

WE SURVIVE THE PASSAGE OF TIME:
← poetry
species
ideas, memories
classical music
paintings, sculptures
literature, poetry
unspoilt landscapes
important discoveries
and inventions
← unspoilt landscape

[B] Go on to consider why it is that certain things survive the passage of time (for example, some music, art forms, wilderness areas, etc.) while others do not. This is helping to focus the children's minds on the key concepts of why certain things change in the world around us, how they change, and whether change is inevitable. An interesting wall display on which to mount writing on this complex subject could depict a crystal ball alongside a scientist to represent the fact that some changes are predictable and, inevitably, others are not.

Activity 4: Stories of changes

[A] Write stories (with newspaper headline-style titles) telling of sudden and dramatic changes that the world or people endure, such as 'Earthquake devastates California', 'Ten die in bomb blast', 'Lost daughter reunited with parents', 'Lightning strikes farmworker', 'Local mother gives birth to quads', 'War hero returns after 48 years', 'Freedom for hostages', 'Miracle cure for cancer patient', 'Home with a new face – plastic surgery saves life after fire', and so on.

A similar activity would be to scour the popular newspapers for eye-catching headlines from real life which could be assembled as a montage or collage on the theme of change.

[B] The above exercise can be approached as an opportunity for pupils to examine changes – major or

? WHY DO THINGS CHANGE?

HOW DOES THE WORLD CHANGE?

DO ALL THINGS CHANGE?

HOW DO WE KNOW WHAT WILL CHANGE?

minor – in their own, or their family's, life. If treated with sensitivity, this will give scope for pupils to come to terms with possibly traumatic or unpleasant past experiences and adapting to change.

Activity 5: My revolutionary new invention

Suggest that the children imagine they are world-famous scientists or inventors. Can they dream up and write about an invention that really would change the world and/or people's lives dramatically? Remember to explain what the adjective 'revolutionary' means in this context.

Activity 6: An assembly on 'everyday changes'

Organise an assembly on the theme of everyday changes. Children could act out a series of two-part sketches, the first part showing a new situation and the second part indicating how changes have occurred in this situation with the passage of a few months or a year. For example:

• a family has a new baby. A year later it is constantly crying, and the parents regularly shout at it;
• a farmer sows seeds. A few months later he is celebrating a good harvest;
• a young couple get married. Six months later they are having constant rows;

40

• a man is taken into intensive care after a road accident. A year later he has recovered and is glad to be alive;

• a scientist discovers a new medicine. The formula goes horribly wrong. Several months later a number of people die from taking it.

The message to discuss during this service is that some of the situations go well while others go wrong, often with disastrous results. Consider whether the results were inevitable, or did they happen because of the way people handled the situation? Could each outcome have been different? The key theme of this is to help the children and their audience appreciate that many of life's situations (and to some extent the 'health' of the world) are within our control. Other happenings and outcomes, however, are beyond our control.

Activity 7: The changes of Palm Sunday

Read the following words about Palm Sunday to the children:

Jesus entered Jerusalem knowing what was going to happen during the next few days. We don't really understand why Judas Iscariot, the friend of Jesus, should have betrayed him. But we know how very easy it sometimes is to let our friends down, or to be disloyal to them. We imagine Jesus must have felt very lonely when all his friends ran away and left him. We know what it is like to feel lonely, especially when we have been let down by people.

Judas identifies Jesus with a kiss

Use this passage as a basis for talking about loyalty and friendship, and emotions felt when we have been let down by someone, or have let someone down ourselves. Write stories and devise cartoon-style sequences called 'The great let down', 'Lost friendship', or 'Betrayal', telling about and depicting being let down by a close

friend. Link this to the previous activity by discussing how, to a certain extent, we can influence the lives and feelings of others by our thoughts, words and actions.

Activity 8: A 'Life cycles' dictionary/card index

Make a class 'Life cycles dictionary' or card index, to include definitions and illustrations of words connected with animal, plant and human life cycles. Add to this as the project progresses, and use it as a reference system. Suggestions of words to include are: adult, conception, egg, embryo, fertilisation, gestation, gene, germination, larva, life cycle, metamorphosis, pupa, sperm. Many others will arise relating to specific creatures and life cycles.

Activity 9: Gifts of newness

A Easter is a time associated with newness as well as beginnings. Discuss with the children how they might give their family and friends a gift of newness. Ask each child to discuss what might be possible, or to write about their ideas. You may need to give suggestions to stimulate further thinking: for example, write a poem and share it with someone, recommend a new book to someone, paint someone a picture, learn a new song to sing at home.

B Discuss the meaning of the phrase 'to turn over a new leaf'. See if the children have ideas as to how they might apply this to their own lives. As an ongoing self-assessment activity, suggest that pupils keep a 'spring cleaning' diary, noting down their responses towards change and thoughts about releasing the old and making room for the new.

C Explore the themes of repentance and renewal within the Christian context of Lent and Easter. Use this as an opportunity to look at festivals of renewal in other religions: for example, Yom Kippur (Judaism) and Diwali (Hinduism) (see **Blueprints** *Festivals* for more information).

MUSIC AND DRAMA

Activity 1: That's life!

Use **Copymaster 1**, (Story of a lifetime) to help children to think through the events that could well happen in an individual's lifetime, and to give practice in sequencing events. This copymaster tells of seven

episodes of a fictitious person's life, beginning with his birth. The events are in jumbled order. Ask the children to read the boxes on the copymaster, cut all material out, then collate it in the correct order to form a booklet, with additional writing or drawing intersecting the 'pages'. Alternatively, children could write a much more comprehensive story of Francis Cooper's life, taking the events given as a basis for elaboration, describing them in much greater detail and telling of events in this person's life that happened in between the key episodes given. Again, one of the basic messages of this activity is that events come and go in our lives: some are within our control and others are not, but inevitably life goes on – we grow and become older, and circumstances change through the years. In the words of Gilbert and Sullivan:

Try we life-long, we can never
Straighten out life's tangled skein,
Why should we in vain endeavour,
Guess and guess and guess again?

Life's a pudding full of plums,
Care's a canker that benumbs.
Life's a pudding full of plums,
Care's a canker that benumbs.
Wherefore waste our elocution
On impossible solution?
Life's a pleasant institution,
Let us take it as it comes!
(Quintet from Act 1 of *The Gondoliers*)

Invite groups of children to write out their own verses along similar lines and set these to 'operatic'-style music, experimenting with a variety of instruments. Build on the theme of 'A portrait of a life' by devising a drama or 'operatic' show on change and perform this to other classes.

SCIENCE

C2–6

Activity 1: Life cycles of butterflies and moths

A Study the life cycles of butterflies and moths, if possible by acquiring some eggs or larvae for the classroom and providing the conditions necessary for their growth and development. These may be collected in their natural habitats, or acquired from specialist suppliers of biological material, who will also advise on housing, feeding and additional reference material to inform your studies. Addresses are provided in the resources section of this book. Whether or not you are able to rear some butterflies or moths yourself, the children should be fascinated to learn more about the amazing life transitions which these creatures have.

Background information
Butterflies and moths start life as eggs, and go through some substantial changes before they reach adulthood. Both belong to the order of *Lepidoptera*, which means 'scaly wings'. They are insects and have (as adults) three body parts, six legs and two sets of wings. Life changes are called a complete metamorphosis, involving transitions from egg to larva to pupae to adult.

B Draw and paint large charts for the classroom wall, showing the difference between butterflies and moths. Begin by helping the children to list the differences, and then they can be written out in poster form.

Note Butterfly and moth templates in Section 3 may be helpful.

C Use **Copymaster 2** (Life cycle of a butterfly) to help children learn more about the various stages of a butterfly's life. Let pupils research the stages shown, write about them, and colour the illustrations. If possible, observe butterflies in their natural habitat or arrange a visit to a local butterfly farm.

Background information
Stages shown in the copymaster are as follows:

1) The butterfly lays her eggs on plant leaves (she then dies).

BUTTERFLIES	MOTHS
Thin body	Fatter, furry body
Fly by day	Fly at night
Rest with wings erect	Rest with wings flat
Larva attaches itself to a support and changes to pupa known as a chrysalis.	Larvae form pupae in the ground or on dead leaves. Others spin a cocoon within which to form a pupa.

Can you tell a butterfly from a moth?

2) Caterpillars hatch from the eggs.
3) Caterpillars feed regularly, usually on the plant on which they hatched.
4) Caterpillars shed their skins several times as they grow.
5) When fully grown, caterpillars stop eating and secure themselves by a thread of silk.
6) Caterpillars turn into a pupa or chrysalis, with a harder skin.
7) In time, the chrysalis begins to open and the adult butterfly emerges.
8) The adult spreads its wings to dry them, and soon takes flight.

Activity 2: The life cycle of a plant

A Help children to learn about the parts of a plant, and to understand that plants also have life cycles. No doubt pupils will be familiar with some aspects of plant life, such as seed growth, but they may not be familiar

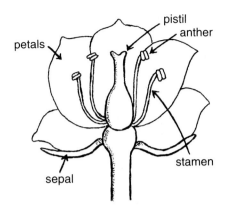

with complete life cycles. Large diagrams to show the parts of a flowering plant could be drawn, painted or created from needlecraft techniques.

B Make a detailed study of seeds. Take a large seed, such as a broad bean, and cut it in half to view the parts which make up the bean. Make labelled sketches of these parts.

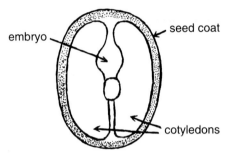

Broad bean: a dicotyledon

Background information
Seeds consist of an outside layer or seed coat, an embryo and one or two cotyledons. Seeds with one cotyledon are called monocotyledons, and seeds with two are known as dicotyledons. The cotyledons are the seed's source of food, which enables growth during germination. The embryo is the part of the seed which develops into the plant. The seed coat protects these vital internal parts against damage.

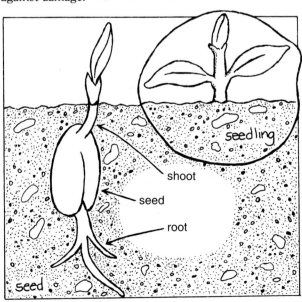

From seed to seedling

C Follow on from the above activity by growing some broad bean seeds and observing growth of the shoots and root. Broad beans germinate easily and will do so in water so that the children can observe what is happening. Wedge them in a see-through container between a roll of blotting paper and the side of the container. If possible, plant seedlings in soil, and maintain observation of growth so that the children can see the development of stem and leaves.

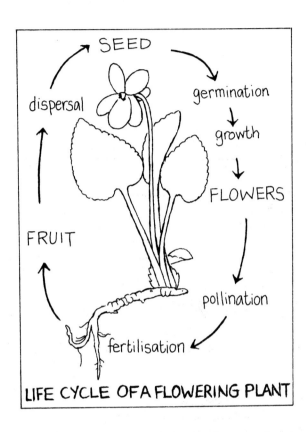

LIFE CYCLE OF A FLOWERING PLANT

The key teaching point in all this is, of course, that the seedling grows into a mature plant which produces flowers and seeds of its own. If possible, germinate a variety of seeds and monitor their development to maturity. Make diagrams – which could be simply written or, better still, illustrated – to show the life cycle of flowering plants that have been grown.

D As an integral part of the above process, it will be necessary to discuss and investigate key concepts, including conditions necessary for growth (light, warmth, moisture and nutrients), the sexual organs within flowers (pollen grains and ovules) and the process of pollination. Numerous books are available on these subjects for further reference. Older pupils can be engaged in practical investigations, such as growing seeds in varient conditions to discover the effects of light, warmth and moisture on them; investigating pollen grains and ovules by taking apart a large flower; and studying pollination in the field by observing the activity of bees and other insects in the summer time. The following diagrams should be helpful as background material and can be elaborated upon by the children.

Background information
The sexual parts within a flower are as illustrated below:

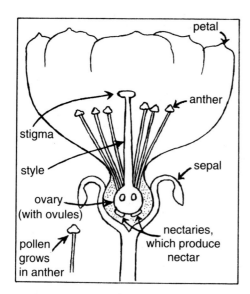

Sexual parts within a flower

Pollination occurs when the insect reaches into the flower to collect nectar: as it does so, pollen rubs off on to its body. When it travels to another flower, pollen is transferred from the insect's body to the stigma. In the ovary, pollen grains fertilise with the ovule.

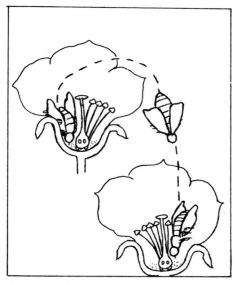

The pollination of a flower

E Use **Copymaster 3** (Plant life cycles) as a matching game to help reinforce the key idea that phases of a plant's life are related. Provide children with additional reference material on flowers and trees, and ask them to match each seed shown with its leaf and flower.

Background information
The six plants shown are: horse chestnut tree; nasturtium; English oak tree; sweet pea; bean; sunflower.

F Go out on a field investigation and ask the children to collect examples of various stages in the life cycle of plants – seeds, leaves (one carefully removed) and petals (remove only one, not the whole flower). Back in the classroom, display these as sets and in the correct sequence, perhaps following the pattern of the life cycle diagram above (see item **C**).

Activity 3: Animal life cycles – the frog
A Investigate animal life cycles. The life cycle of a frog is a common but useful starting point as this creature demonstrates a complete cycle from egg (spawn) to young (tadpole) to adults, with fascinating changes as these stages go by. If you intend to rear tadpoles in the classroom, do pay attention to conservation. Frogspawn should never be removed from a 'wild' pond. Collect a little from a garden pond in circumstances where the owner gives an assurance that frogs are plentiful. Always ensure that the young frogs reared in captivity are returned to their native habitat once the children have completed their observations of the transition from tadpole to frog.

B **Copymaster 4** (Life cycle of a frog) provides a set of useful illustrations of the frog's life cycle for the children to colour, write about and match to their observations of real amphibians. Ideally, visit a pond on several occasions to make observations in the field.
   A key teaching point here is that not all members of the animal kingdom go through the same series of stages as the frog. As an associated task, teach children that frogs belong to the animal group named amphibians, which have particular characteristics. These could be written out alongside paintings of frogs and other amphibians.

Background information
•   Amphibians spend periods of their lives on land and other periods in water.
•   Their immature stages are spent in or near water.
•   Their skin is moist and porous: this assists in breathing.
•   They make sounds by forcibly sending out air from lungs.
•   They absorb moisture through their skin.
•   They are cold blooded.

C Go out on field investigations and look for evidence of other animal (including mammals, birds and invertebrates) life cycles. Emphasise that all living creatures have a life cycle of some sort – that is, they go through a number of changes from conception or fertilisation to maturity. Before eventually dying, mature adults are able to reproduce their species. Signs to look for, closely observe and record in the field include eggs of different kinds (both hard-shelled and others), insects in various life stages, and evidence of nests of various kinds.
   Use **Copymaster 5** (Animal life cycles) as a recording sheet for field observations of animal life cycles. Ensure that pupils write the date of their observations. Ideally

visits should be made throughout the year, or at least throughout the duration of the topic in spring/early summer, so that variations can be noted. The rest of the sheet can then be completed as follows: in the left-hand column, note the sign observed (egg, dead insect, etc.); in the next column, record the precise location of this sign, and in the third column, the life stage of this find. Finally, pupils can sketch the sign or make any other relevant notes to aid identification or sketching later. When pupils have completed Copymaster 5, they can undertake a project on the wildlife of a specific location, using the information they have gathered as a class.

Activity 4: The human life cycle

Extend work on animal life cycles by helping pupils to begin to learn about human reproduction. This could simply involve a study of how a human foetus develops within its mother's body until a living baby is born which gradually grows to maturity. With older children the subject of evolution can be pursued, leading to some elementary understanding of how the natural world and life forms have evolved through time, and the fact that they will continue to change in the future.

A **Copymaster 6** (Human embryo) provides an opportunity for researching about the development of a human baby inside its mother. The sheet shows six stages of development but in an incorrect order. Provide children with a copymaster and scissors. They can cut out the drawings, rearrange them in the correct order and glue them on to another sheet of paper or card, adding labels or fuller descriptions of what each stage shows and its approximate age.

Background information

The correct order of pictures is as follows:
- Picture F – Age two weeks after conception. Eyes of the embryo begin to develop.
- Picture D – Age six weeks after conception. The embryo now resembles a human being, with the beginnings of ears, hands and feet. Its heart starts beating.
- Picture E – Age ten weeks after conception. The baby can move its arms and legs. Fingers and toes begin to grow.
- Picture A – Age 18 weeks after conception. The baby has fingernails and starts to move and 'kick' within the womb.
- Picture B – Age 30 weeks after conception. Internal organs are now functioning or ready to function.
- Picture C – Age 38 to 40 weeks (nine months) after conception. The baby is fully developed and ready to be born, and separated from the mother's umbilical cord.

B Human reproduction and basic life processes could well be linked to work on genetics, the fact that information in the form of genes is passed on from one generation to the next. Make pictures of human cells, either accurate drawings or more creative art work, showing their key components.

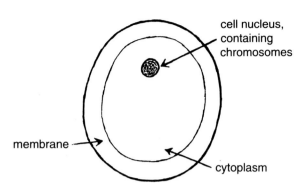

Key components of human cells

Background information

Cells which make up the female egg and male sperm contain a set of 'instructions' that determine the physical characteristics of the baby: for example, eye and hair colour. These instructions or genes are carried in the cell's chromosomes inside its nucleus. Every human embryo has 46 chromosomes, 23 of which are derived from the mother and 23 from the father. Some 10 000 genes are carried on each chromosome. The egg and sperm both carry chromosomes. The egg carries a variety called X chromosomes. The sperm carries half X chromosomes and half of a variety known as Y chromosomes. At the point of conception, if the egg meets X chromosomes then a girl is conceived: if the egg meets Y chromosomes, then a boy is conceived.

C Design conception diagrams to illustrate the above process.

D Suggest that the children undertake an investigation of genetics and inheritance in their own families. Each child should survey his or her own eye (or hair) colour and that of his or her parents, grandparents,

45

brothers and sisters, if this is possible. Let them devise original charts or other methods of recording. See what patterns emerge. Consider other human characteristics: discuss, for example, whether face shape, general build and personality seem to have any genetic links.

Note This activity should be treated with sensitivity if any class members live with carers other than their biological parents, are from single parent homes or have few relatives to survey.

Activity 5: Lifecycles and change

A Make a study of gestation periods. Research these from reference books or consult 'experts' such as farmers who work regularly with animals and need to know when pregnant mothers will give birth. Display results of research in illustrative form.

Gestation periods

B Extend this work on the concept of life cycles and change yet further by considering the evolution of species, and the evidence we have for this in fossil form. Consult some of the many excellent reference books available on these subjects. Let the children paint illustrations of the key stages in the evolution of life on earth, and display these in the correct order with accompanying writing, giving practice in sequencing.

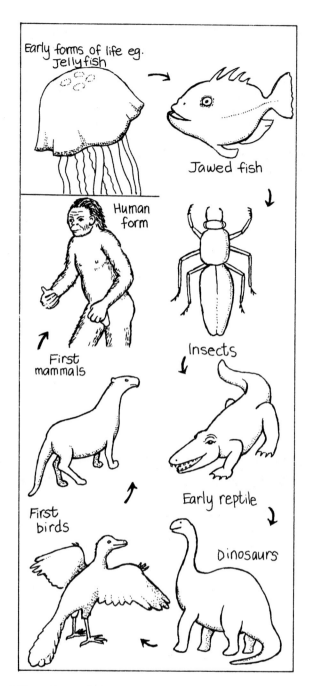

Life cycles and change

Background information
Life on earth is constantly changing, though these changes may be imperceptible in a short timespan. As chromosomes are passed on from one generation to another (in both animals and plant life) slight changes occur in their structure and new characteristics are inherited. Sometimes the species in question becomes stronger as a result, and more able to survive on earth; sometimes species or members become weaker, and may even die out altogether.

C Suggest that the children research related subjects such as extinct forms of life, the life and work of Charles Darwin, and the evidence about changes in life forms that is available to us today.

46

D Let the children work in groups to make 'life cycle cards' so that a matching game can be played. At a simple level, make two cards for each species, one with an embryonic life form on it and one bearing the adult form. Children can then play a game of matching these cards in the same way that 'snap' is played.

Elaborate the above activity by incorporating cards representing plant life cycles, or by making three or four cards from each species, so that children have to sort them into sets.

Life cycle 'snap!' cards

ART AND TECHNOLOGY

Activity 1: A butterfly collage

A Make large colourful collages of butterflies for display. Link to science by using this activity to help teach children the parts of a butterfly. Beautiful pictures could also be made using needlecraft techniques, perhaps sewing on sequins for wing decorations.

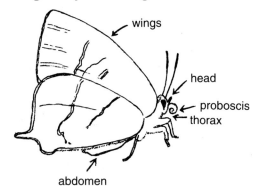

B Construct three-dimensional pictures of butterflies on flowers. Let the children draw, colour and cut out butterflies on thick card, with a flap measured to fit slots in their background picture. Paint a background of large colourful flowers on thin card or stiff paper. Cut slots in the flowers in which to insert the flaps on the butterflies, so that the insects appear to have settled on the flowers.

C Older children can attempt to design and make a simple butterfly kite using lightweight Cellophane® and tissue spread over a balsa wood frame.

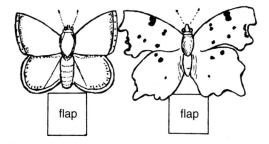

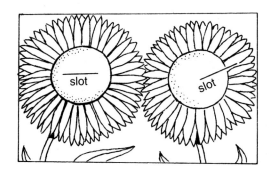

Activity 2: Life cycle collages

Make life cycle needlecraft collages. Cut a large circle of felt as a base, and divide with rick-rack braid or embroidery stitches into four quadrants. Appliqué designs in each section to show your chosen plant or animal life cycle, adding further embroidery stitches for elaboration. Mount the completed design on stiff card and hang on the wall.

47

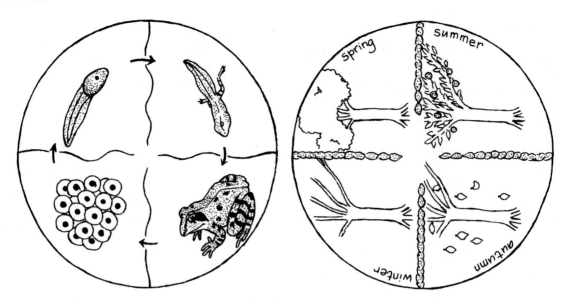

Children will have fun making needlecraft collages

Activity 3: Frogspawn pictures and collages

Make pictures of frogspawn. Glue some tall grasses on to a suitable background, or cut artificial reeds from stiff paper. Print white circles in a random distribution between them, or glue on circles of white paper (kitchen film covering these makes an authentic spawn). Add embryonic tadpoles cut from black felt or paper. These can then be stuck on to a background 'pond' cut from silver foil and blue paper. Paint pond weeds to decorate the scene, with cut-out frogs nestling between them.

B Cut a segment shape out of polystyrene or alternative printing block, and print in vivid green or other suitable colours on to a background made from leafy wallpaper samples. Add painted heads and legs to your caterpillars.

Activity 4: Caterpillar pictures

A Caterpillars make wonderful subjects for creative art work – they could be painted as giant-sized larvae, and mounted against a background of printed leaves.

Activity 5: Happy families

Paint pictures of 'families', reminding pupils of their work on embryology and human reproduction. Suggest that the children paint a mother, father and young of each species selected. These could then be displayed on a wall frieze depicting families of various kinds. While this is suggested under art activities, a key teaching point is that all families require a male and a female in order to produce offspring. It is also a useful activity for teaching vocabulary associated with adults and young.

woman , child , man   duck , duckling , drake   cow , bull , calf

Family pictures

Story of a lifetime

Two-year-old killed in a road accident

A car crashed into a tree on the ice-covered A167 killing a 2-year-old passenger. Rebecca, daughter of Francis and Georgina Cooper of Newburn, died instantly.

Junior League results

Mountjoy School claimed a hard-won victory over rivals Eastleigh in Saturday's Junior Football League. Francis Cooper led the Mountjoy team to a 1–0 victory, scoring in the last five minutes of play.

Births

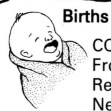

COOPER To Georgina and Francis, twins Hugo and Rebecca, born 1 October, Newburn.

Golden wedding story

Francis and Georgina Cooper of Newburn celebrated their golden wedding anniversary in splendid style. The party was attended by son Hugo, and family and friends from the UK and USA.

COOPER
To Laura and Edward, a son, Francis, born 6 June, Newburn.

Marriage of local football star

Local football hero Francis Cooper married Californian Georgina Moxon in a Pacific View wedding last week. The couple met while Francis was touring the USA with the England football team.

Deaths

COOPER, F. E.
Francis Cooper of Newburn died peacefully after a short illness, aged 86 years. He will be sadly missed by wife Georgina and son Hugo.

Frank

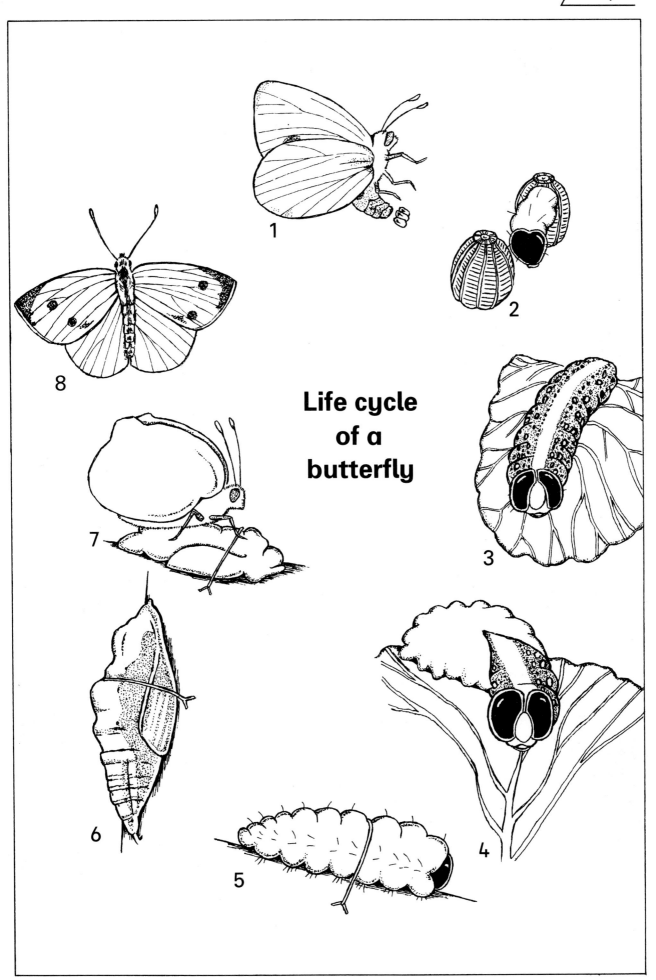

**Life cycle
of a
butterfly**

Life cycles C2

Plant life cycles

Seeds, leaves and flowers – can you put these into sets?

Draw lines to link parts of the same plant.

Life cycles C3

Life cycle of a frog

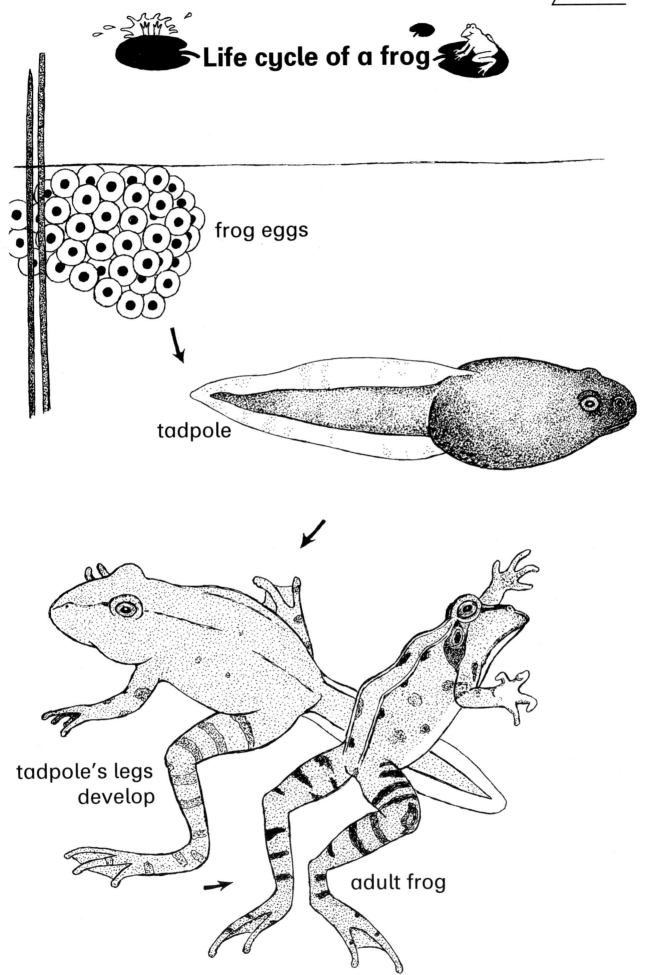

frog eggs

tadpole

tadpole's legs
develop

adult frog

53

Animal life cycles

Name _____   Date _____

Sign	Location	Life stage	Sketch/further notes

54   **Life cycles C5**

Human embryo

What is the correct order for these pictures?

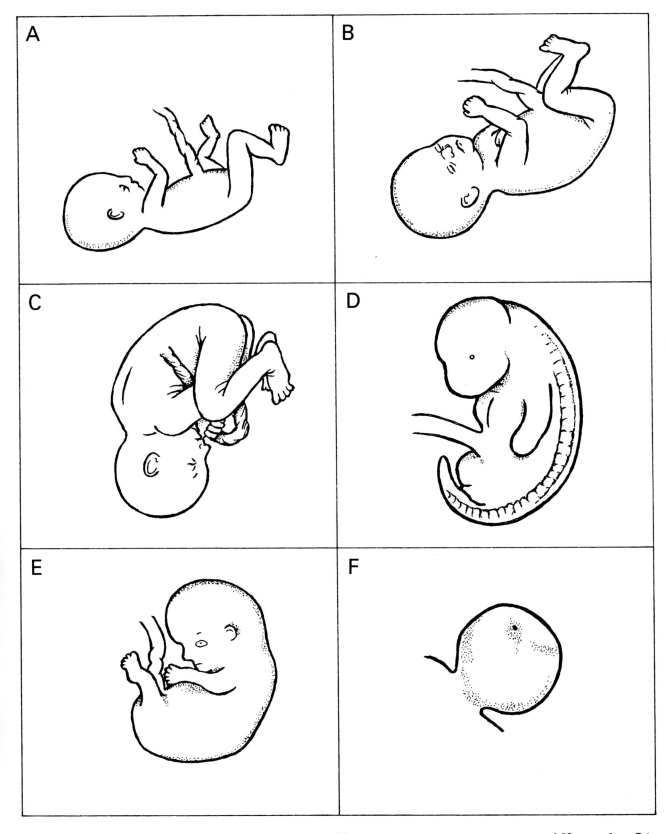

Life cycles C6

SECTION 2
Services and
Assemblies

Trees: An Easter assembly

INTRODUCTION

The following suggestions are for an Easter assembly or service based on the theme of trees. It would be ideal for presentation by a class which had been undertaking a spring term topic on trees, incorporating a study of those which feature in the Easter story.

The purpose of the words which follow is to provide an outline for a service, with the incorporation of appropriate background material. The wording can, of course, be adapted to suit the age group of readers with whom it is being used. Many of the readings have been written by children themselves, who were aged 10 when the service was first created and conducted. These are indicated by the words 'pupil script'. Teachers may wish to substitute original material on the same themes written by their own pupils where this is appropriate.

No attempt is made to divide the script into parts. The term 'narrator' is used throughout. Presumably, teachers will allow as many children as possible the opportunity to participate as readers by dividing up the narrative into suitable sections. Suggestions for appropriate hymns are provided, though of course other hymns or songs may be substituted.

The only props needed for this service are paintings or large pictures of the trees discussed – the palm, the dogwood and the olive. These can be mounted behind the narrators and indicated at appropriate times in the service.

Date palm

Dogwood

Olive

Pupil script:

Palm Sunday

Palm Sunday is the day when Jesus rode into Jerusalem on a donkey. When he arrived, the streets were lined with people. One man shouted 'Hosanna! Blessed is he that comes in the name of the Lord'. Then everyone started shouting 'Hosanna!' People climbed up the palm trees to get a better view. Some people laid their coats in the road as a sign of respect. Others were taking the branches off the palm trees and waving them very excitedly. Everyone was so happy, and greeting their king. Only Jesus himself knew that death was near.

Pupil script:

The palm tree

One proverb says 'He who plants the palm will never live to eat its fruit'. This is because the palm is a very slow growing tree. It could take about a hundred years before it starts giving fruit.

The date palm usually grows in tropical lands and is very common in Palestine. The leaves can grow up to about four metres long. As the tree grows the bottom leaves fall off, leaving marks on the trunk. The trunk is tall and slender. A date palm has not got any annual rings. In the tropical areas, the date palm is one of the main food supplies. Date palms can stand a lot of heat but will die without moisture.

Narrator: So, here was the Palm tree, in the midst of all the excitement of Jesus arriving in Jerusalem. What a day of glory for the palm!

Pupil script:

The glory of the palm tree
Hosanna! Hosanna!
The King is coming.
Everybody, lay your coats down for the Lord.
Wave palm leaves to our King.

Trees: An Easter Assembly

Narrator: Easter time is here again. We wish you all a happy day, and a happy Easter holiday.

Class X has spent a lot of time this term learning about trees. We have learned that trees are very important things in our world.

There are many good reasons why we should all take care of trees: for example, they are beautiful to look at and give us a lot of pleasure; they provide wood for many of our needs; they breathe oxygen into the air for us to breathe; they provide houses for many birds and insects.

[*Other examples can be added here. A large illustration could be painted for each reason given, and held up as a poster for the school to see as the list is read.*]

Prayer: *A tree lover's prayer*

Dear Heavenly Father, we thank you for your wonderful gift of the beauty of trees. Please help us to protect all trees from inconsiderate people, and help us to realise the great importance of trees in the world. We love the sweet smelling perfume of blossom in springtime, the glorious green crowns of summer, the brilliant shades of gold and bronze in autumn, and the majestic silhouettes standing stark against a winter sky. Help us, Lord, to encourage everyone to be a tree lover and to appreciate this wonderful gift. Amen.

Narrator: You might be thinking, 'What has all this got to do with Easter?' Well, believe it or not, trees have an important part to play in the story of what happened at the first Eastertime. Two thousand years ago, Jesus, the Son of God, died a cruel death, nailed to a cross, and every Easter we remember the story of his death. The last week of the life of Jesus began on a Sunday, named Palm Sunday.

[*This would be an appropriate place to introduce the idea of palm crosses. Reference could be made to the fact that many Christian churches distribute these to the people on Palm Sunday as a reminder of Jesus' entry into Jerusalem, or palm crosses could be made by the class for distribution to the school at the end of the service. Details of how to make palm crosses will be found on p. 94.*]

Narrator: The excitement and glory was not to last for long. In the crowd, Jesus also had enemies. He knew, and they knew, that in a few days he would be dead.

On the Thursday after Palm Sunday, Jesus met with his twelve disciples for the last time. They had a simple meal together, and after they had eaten, Jesus said, 'One of you is going to betray me'. That meant that one of his friends was going to let him down, to tell the soldiers where they could find him, and capture him.

Who was it to be? The answer was Judas. Judas Iscariot – once a friend, now a traitor. And so, thanks to Judas, Jesus was captured and taken for trial before Pontius Pilate.

In the New English Bible, St John tells us that part of the story.

Reading: The troops with their commander, and the Jewish police, now arrested Jesus and secured him. They took him first to Annas. Annas was father-in-law of Caiaphas, the High Priest for that year – the same Caiaphas who had advised the Jews that it would be in their interest if one man died for the whole people.

The High Priest questioned Jesus about his disciples and about what he taught. Jesus replied, 'I have spoken openly to all the world; I have always taught in the synagogue and in the temple, where all Jews congregate; I have said nothing in secret. Why question me? Ask my hearers what I told them; they know what I said'.

So Annas sent him bound to Caiaphas, the High Priest. From Caiaphas, Jesus was led into the

---

Climb up the palm trees to get a better view.
Lay palms down in the road
For Christ's donkey to walk on.
Hosanna!
The King is here!
The palms and people celebrate together.

Pupil script: *The glory of the palm tree*
A rush of excitement,
Echoes of laughter,
Greeting the Lord.
Palm leaves everywhere,
Coats thrown to the floor.
'Hosanna!' was heard a thousand times.
A glorious day for the palm tree,
Being used as a ladder
To get a better view,
Used as a banner
Leaves fill the air,
Waving, fluttering,
Majestic palm
Your hour of glory is here.

Pupil script: *The glory of the palm tree*
'Hosanna!' was the cry
From joyous crowds.
The dusty road lay clad in cloaks,
Age-old stood the palm.
Waving branches greeted the Lord,
Lush green leaves of the palm.
A glorious day.
People climbing the towering trunk,
Scrambling, their Lord to see.
What a joyous day for the old palm tree!

Hymn: *All Glory, Laud and Honour to Thee, Redeemer King*

Governor's headquarters . . . . Pilate went out to them and asked, 'What charge do you bring against this man?' 'If he were not a criminal', they replied, 'we should not have brought him before you'. Pilate said, 'Take him away and try him by your own law'. The Jews answered, 'We are not allowed to put any man to death'.

Pilate then went back into his headquarters and summoned Jesus. 'Are you the King of the Jews?' he asked. Jesus replied, 'My kingdom does not belong to this world. If it did, my followers would be fighting to save me from arrest by the Jews. My task is to bear witness to the truth. For this I was born; for this I came into the world, and all who are not deaf to truth hear my voice'.

Pilate went out again to the Jews. 'For my part', he said, 'I find no case against him. But you have a custom that I release one prisoner for you at Passover. Would you like me to release the King of the Jews?' Again the clamour rose: 'Not him; we want Barabbas!' (Barabbas was a bandit.)

Pilate now took Jesus and had him flogged; and the soldiers plaited a crown of thorns and placed it on his head, and robed him in a purple cloak. Once more Pilate came out and said to the Jews, 'Here he is'; I am bringing him out to let you know that I find no case against him'; and Jesus came out wearing the crown of thorns and the purple cloak. 'Behold the Man', said Pilate. The chief priests and their henchmen saw him and shouted 'Crucify! Crucify!'

From that moment Pilate tried hard to release him; but the Jews kept shouting, 'If you let this man go, you are no friend to Caesar; any man who claims to be a king is defying Caesar'. They shouted 'Away with him! Away with him! Crucify him!' 'Crucify your king?' said Pilate. 'We have no king but Caesar', the Jews replied. Then at last, to satisfy them, he handed Jesus over to be crucified.

Narrator: So the Son of God was taken to be crucified, to be nailed to a wooden cross.

Hymn: *There is a Green Hill Far Away*

Narrator: Nailed to a wooden cross was he. And where did that come from? From a tree!

[*Point to dogwood.*]

A living tree, the home of animals, birds and insects – now to be cut down, and used for the cruelest death in the history of the world.

There is a legend telling that the tree used to make the cross was a dogwood tree. We have painted a picture of it. It was very large, just like the oak, with a massive trunk and a huge crown. A very strong tree.

We have tried to imagine how the poor dogwood must have felt at being used to crucify the Lord. All its life taken away – chopped down, carved into a cross, a death weapon.

Pupil script *The dogwood's tragedy*

Why me?
To share the tragedy of my Lord's death,
My life has ended
All my leaves and flowers dead.
My branches make the cross.
Why me?
I stand stark and helpless,
The nails penetrating my branches.
Forgive me, Lord, I mean you no harm.
I die with you,
The agony,
The tragedy,
Why me?

Pupil script: *The dogwood's tragedy*
What evil have I done
To deserve this heartbreak?
Blood is dripping all over me.
The Lord's dry skin is covered in my splinters.
I am chosen to do this evil.
His heartbeats diminish,
His breath is slow.
The shadow of death is near.
O Lord, forgive me,
I know you are innocent and the Son of God.
Why me? Why me?
Once I was a supplier of food, of homes,
Of shelter.
My blossom was beautiful and bright.
I gave life.
I was life.
Now abruptly, I become a tree of death.

Narrator: But the legend of the dogwood also tells us that Jesus felt sorry for the dogwood and knew that the tree was sad. So he said:

Pupil script: *Jesus' reply to the dogwood*
You don't deserve to be killed with me.
I feel sorry for you, dogwood,
And I will change your appearance for ever,
So that people will never forget
That you have shared my death.
I will make your trunk short and slender
Instead of wide and dense.
Each of the flowers of your blossom
Will be in the shape of a cross.
It will have four petals, two long and two short.
The middle of each flower
Will resemble a crown of thorns.
The edges of your petals will appear rusty and bloodstained,
A reminder of the nails
Driven through my hands into your wood.
I will remember you always,
And will remind the people that
You suffered with me.

Pupil script: *The dogwood's tragedy*
Why am I here?
Why should I suffer?
My once radiant branches
Transformed into a deadly cross.
A multitude of trees,
But why me?
The agony of death.
I am killing my Lord.
I want to weep,
But I cannot.
Blood drips from my dingy branches.
Pain is eating my heart.
Bloodstained and weathered,
I bear the shadow of death.
The last breath is drawn.
He is dead,
And I die too.

Narrator: And so, from that day onwards, the dogwood was no longer an enormous forest tree. Today it is short and slender. So Christ died. His body was taken down from the cross and placed in a tomb. The end of a life.

[*Pause: reflective music.*]

Yet that end is only a part of our story. For, just like the reawakening of dead life in springtime, when buds come on the trees and we are reminded that life can have a new beginning, so the world was to be shown that Jesus was to have a new life.
And so we look at our last tree – the olive tree.

63

Pupil script: *The olive trees in the Garden of Gethsemane*
The olive tree is very important in our Easter story, because many olive trees grew in the Garden of Gethsemane – and that was the place where Jesus' body was taken to be buried. The English translation of the word 'Gethsemane' is 'the place of the oil press', telling us that it was planted with olive trees, because olive trees were very very important for giving oil to the people.

Pupil script: *The olive tree*
The olive tree is a shrub, though some may grow as high as twenty to thirty feet. The oil from olive trees comes from its fruit. The fruit of the olive tree is about half the size of a plum. The olives are green, but when they are ripe they are black. The fruit is crushed by bare feet or by an olive press. Every two years an olive tree will produce about six gallons (or 48 pints) of oil. The oil is used for cooking, skin cleaning, anointing, medicine, and for burning in oil-lamps. The person who owned the Garden of Gethsemane was Joseph of Arimathaea. He must have been a wealthy man to own so many olive trees.

Narrator: And so it was the olive tree in the Garden of Gethsemane that was to witness what happened three days after Jesus' body was placed in the tomb. We have imagined that the olive tree tells of what it saw on that first Easter Sunday morning.

Pupil script: *The day of the resurrection*
Dawn is breaking.
Mary is walking in sadness,
Wanting to be near her Lord.
The boulder is moved.
Mary is weeping tears of sadness.
Her Lord is gone.
'Why are you crying?'
A heavenly voice is saying.
'My son is missing.'
'Why are you crying?'
Another voice is saying softly,
'Mary.'
Thinking it was the gardener, she replied,
'If you have taken his body,
Tell me where to,
Then I will take him.'
The man is speaking again, saying
'Mary.'
Excitement is filling Mary's body.
She is overjoyed and thrilled.
Happiness has returned to Mary.
She is running towards Jesus.
'Oh, do not touch me,' he is saying.
Joy is in her heart.
She runs to tell the disciples.
Everyone is rejoicing.

Pupil script: *The day of resurrection*
Dawn is breaking.
There stands Mary.
The rock has been moved.
Mary is weeping,
And the angels ask, 'Why are you crying?'
'Jesus' body has been stolen.'
Then she hears a voice.
Mary thinks it is the gardener,
And she says, 'If you have stolen the body
Please let me know where he is.'
Then he says, 'Mary.'
Mary recognises the voice –
Her own master,
Risen from the dead.

Pupil script: *The day of resurrection*
Dawn appears.
How unhappy Mary looks
As she walks to sit with her saviour.
A flash of horror
Shows in her face
When she finds the boulder has been moved.
'Someone has stolen my Lord!'
She quickly turns away and weeps.
'Why are you weeping?'
She turns and finds two angels in the tomb.
'Fear not.'
'Someone has stolen my Lord,' Mary says.
She sees a man.
'If you have taken him,
Tell me where he is, and I will take him.'
'Mary,' was the reply.
'Master!' shouted Mary, 'My own Lord.'
There stood Jesus, radiant,
Risen from the dead.

Narrator: This wonderful day teaches us that death is simply a new beginning, not an end. Jesus came back to life to show us this. He died for every person that ever lived, that is alive now, and that will live on earth. He truly was the Son of God, and he is alive in our hearts today.

Prayers: Let us pray
Dear God, we are very happy to know that Jesus, having died for us on the cross, was raised again alive on the first Easter Sunday morning. We thank you that this means we can know and love a saviour who is alive in our hearts today and for ever. Amen.

Help us, Lord, as we look forward to the Easter holidays, not to forget the real meaning of Easter – the sadness of Good Friday and the joy of Easter Day. We thank you for your great love to us. Amen.

Hymn: *The Strife is O'er, The Battle Done*

65

The Easter story

INTRODUCTION

The following pages contain words outlining the key events of the first Easter, which could be adapted for use with children in a variety of ways. The story is presented within the framework of a service, so that readers could lead a school assembly, taking the audience through the story and interspersing narrative with hymns, prayers and pupils' own creative writing at appropriate points. Indications are given in the text below of where these might be included. Some examples of pupils' writing by Key Stage 2 children are also provided, though clearly you may wish to substitute original writing from your own pupils at various stages in the unfolding of the story.

An alternative use of the text below is as a resource for telling children of the Christian story of Easter. Substantial passages could be read aloud or photocopied for the pupils to read themselves.

If it is your intention to use the complete text as a service or assembly, you will need to prepare the introductory picture with the children.

You will need:

- a large piece of black card;
- candle wax (melted);
- a stiff paint brush;
- two colour washes – blue and green powder paint mixed thinly with water.

What to do:

Melt the candle wax. While this is gradually liquifying, prepare the card by drawing the outline of three crosses on a hillside in pencil. Paint wax over the area of the crosses, and leave it to dry. Erase the pencil lines. When the service is under way, the narrator who is conducting this part of it should paint the sky area with the blue wash and the hillside with the green wash; of course, the crosses will mysteriously resist the wax and stand out as black shapes on the hill. Prop up the card on an easel before the service begins.

The Easter Story

Narrator: Good morning. Today we are going to tell you a special story. I will begin by painting a picture – not a usual sort of picture, but a very mysterious one. A sheet of card, some paint and a brush – that is all I need.

[*Child paints picture and reveals crosses.*]

So the mysterious picture is revealed. The story that this picture is about is even more mysterious. It helps to explain why the death of one person a long time ago was so important. Three crosses on a hillside.

[*Child points to picture.*]

This is the cross of Christ, the Son of God.

[*Child points to central cross.*]

Jesus ended his life in a scene like this; the end of the life of the person who was born as a baby in a manger in Bethlehem.

Born to play
Born to preach
Born to teach
Born to die, to save the world.

So important was the life and death of Jesus, that we are going to remember the events of the last few days that he lived.

Hymn: [*An appropriate hymn, such as A Man for All the People could be sung here.*]

The story of Palm Sunday

Jesus and his disciples joined the crowds of people going to Jerusalem for the Passover festival. He sent two disciples on ahead, telling them what to do. They were to go to a nearby village and fetch a donkey, telling the owner that Jesus needed it. No one had ever ridden this donkey before, but when Jesus sat on its back it stood very still. Jesus rode it into Jerusalem.

The crowd heard that Jesus was coming and flocked to welcome him. They packed the streets and cheered as Jesus rode by, because they were so excited to see him. Some of the crowd threw their cloaks onto the road to make a carpet. Others broke off branches from palm trees and waved them like flags, shouting 'Hosanna!' They welcomed Jesus like a king.

Pupil script: Palm Sunday was a very special day, because all the people of Jerusalem were expecting Jesus to arrive. People who lived there were up early, out on the road, waiting for Jesus to come. Pilgrims travelled specially to Jerusalem to watch him. All these people remembered a poem written a long time before, predicting what would happen on that day – that Jesus the King would enter Jerusalem on a donkey, and that the people would shout, wave and be happy. And now that special day had come. And the people waited . . . what a long wait it seemed. Then suddenly, in the distance, they could see a donkey coming along the road, and they knew that Jesus himself would be riding it.

They took off the cloaks they were wearing and laid them down on the road to make a beautiful pathway. Lots of palm trees were growing all around. People pulled off the branches and laid some on the ground for Jesus to walk over. Other branches were waved in the air, and shouts of 'Hosanna!' could be heard. Some people walked in front of Jesus, with others behind, shouting and waving. They called 'Hosanna to the Son of David!'

Hymn: [*For example, All Glory, Laud and Honour to Thee, Redeemer King!*]

Narrator: This ride into Jerusalem marks the beginning of the most important week in the history of the Christian Church. We call this day Palm Sunday. We remember Jesus' ride into Jerusalem on a donkey every year on the Sunday before Easter day.

The story of Jesus' betrayal and trial

Many people were jealous and afraid of Jesus. He was the hero of the people, and leaders of the time were afraid of his power and influence. A plot was organised to kill him. This involved a spy in his group of disciples, Judas Iscariot, who was willing to betray Jesus. Judas was bribed to tell the enemy soldiers where they could find him.

On the evening before Passover, Jesus had a special meal with his disciples, which became known as the Last Supper. Peter and John went to a large upstairs room and got everything ready. When Jesus sat down to the table with his group of twelve friends, they knew that this was the last meal they would share together. When Jesus told them that one of them was a traitor, the disciples were shocked and wondered who this could be. Then Judas got up and ran out of the room. Jesus did not stop him. When Judas had gone, Jesus blessed and broke a loaf of bread. He gave it to his disciples, telling them that his body would be broken like the bread. Then he blessed a cup of wine and passed it round among the disciples, saying that his blood would soon be poured out like the wine. They all knew that Jesus was about to die.

Later that night, in the Garden of Gethsemane, Jesus prayed to God. The disciples were nearby, sleeping. Suddenly there was a noise, and armed soldiers rushed into the garden. Judas ran forward with them and kissed Jesus, showing the soldiers who he was. They grabbed hold of Jesus and took him away, despite attempts by other disciples to stop them.

On Friday morning, the Jewish court presented Jesus to the Roman Governor, named Pontius Pilate. There was a custom at Passover time that one prisoner could be released. Pilate offered to release Jesus because he could not find him guilty of any crime under Roman law. Yet the crowd cried out for another prisoner to

be released: 'We want Barabbas!' Pilate was faced with the rioting crowd and gave in to their wishes. Barabbas the robber was released and Jesus was sentenced to die on a wooden cross with two other prisoners at a place called Golgotha, 'The place of the skull'.

In the Bible, St John tells us this story:

Pilate then went back into his headquarters and summoned Jesus. 'Are you the King of the Jews?' he asked. Jesus replied, 'My kingdom does not belong to this world.'

Pilate said to the people, 'I find no case against this man. But you have a custom that I release one prisoner for you at Passover time. Would you like me to release the King of the Jews?' Again the clamour rose: 'Not him; we want Barabbas!'

Pilate now took Jesus and had him flogged; and the soldiers plaited a crown of thorns and placed it on his head, and robed him in a purple cloak. Then time after time they came up to him crying, 'Hail, King of the Jews!' and struck him on the face. The chief priests saw him and shouted, 'Crucify! Crucify!' 'Take him and crucify him yourselves,' said Pilate, 'for I find no case against him.'

Narrator: It is hard to imagine the atmosphere of the crowd, screaming and shouting for the release of Barabbas – and for the Son of God to be crucified.

Hymn: [For example, There is a Green Hill Far Away.]

The story of the crucifixion

Jesus died a most painful death, nailed to a wooden cross on the hillside at Golgotha. Nailed to the cross above his head was a message, reading 'This is Jesus of Nazareth, King of the Jews'. Jesus was in great pain yet he did not hate the men who had put him to death. 'Father, forgive them,' he prayed. 'They do not know what they are doing.'

In the middle of the day black clouds and darkness covered the country for three hours. At the moment Jesus died, a mighty earthquake shook the land. A watching soldier said, 'Surely this was the Son of God'.

Later that day, a man named Joseph of Arimathaea was given permission to bury Jesus in a tomb in a garden. A huge boulder was rolled in front of the entrance to seal it.

[*Appropriate music, such as the movent known as 'Mars, the Bringer of War' from the Planets Suite by Gustav Holst, can accompany the following Pupil script.*]

Pupil script: *On the cross*
Now is my life's end.
What have I done to make my people angry?
My blood is spilling on to the ground.
I can see the crowd anxious for my departure.
The sun is unbearable.
Everything is a blur.
Sweat runs into my eyes.
Now I am used to the pain, I feel numb.
I am itching all over, but I cannot move my hands.
All my hair is tangled.
The birds are flying above
Ready to savage my body.
Father, why have you forgotten me?
The sun is blinding my eyes, so I cannot see what they are doing below me.
The nails are biting into my flesh.
The rust is eating away my hands.
Father, forgive them, for they don't know what they are doing.
If I look up, the sun blinds me.
If I look down, I see only a blurred crowd.
I close my eyes.
This is now my bitter end.
Father, into your hands I commit my spirit.

Pupil script: *On the cross*
Death is all over my body.
I am burning,
I am aching,
I am fading,
I thirst,
I die.
O Father, why have you forgotten me?
I ask you Father, forgive them, because they do not know what they are doing.
I am fading,
I am burning,
I am aching,
I am ending.
O Father, into your hands I commit my spirit.

Pupil script: *On the cross*
Slowly they push the nails through me,
So slowly . . . .
They laugh and mock me.
I shout out, 'Father, why have you forgotten me?'
Now my body begins to feel like it is splitting.
My body is burning out – like a fire,
Red with misery and pain.
I feel sorry for my enemies.
Father, forgive them, for they do not know what they are doing.
Blood pours over my body.
My skin is dry, very dry.
It seems like my inside is trying to get outside.
My heart is beating so very fast.
Now I feel numb.
I know the shadow of death shall soon cover itself over me.
I hope,
I pray,
Father, into your hands I commit my spirit.

69

I die.

Prayer: Let us pray

Heavenly Father, although we don't understand all about it, we want to thank you for what Jesus did when he died on the cross. We know that he did it for us, so that we could be forgiven and come to you, and we think that it is wonderful that you loved us so much. Help us when we think about Jesus dying on the cross to be truly grateful to him – not taking his act of love for granted, but saying 'thank you' by trying to do the things that please him. For his name's sake. Amen.

Narrator: So Christ died. His body was taken down from the cross and placed in a tomb. Yet that end is only a part of our story. For, just like the reawakening of dead life in springtime, when we are reminded that life can have a new beginning, so the world was to be shown that Jesus was to have a new life.

The story of the resurrection

Two days after Jesus was crucified, Mary of Magdala and some of her friends came to the tomb of Jesus to put spices on his body. They were amazed to find that the boulder which had covered up the tomb entrance had been removed. Their curiosity made them step inside the tomb. To their astonishment sat two angels where the body of Christ had been. Mary started weeping.

'Why are you crying?' asked the angels.

Mary replied 'Because someone has taken my Lord from his tomb.'

Then Mary saw a shadow behind her in the garden. She turned, still weeping, and thought that the figure she saw was the gardener. She asked him, 'Have you taken my Lord away? If so, please, please tell me where you have put his body.'

The figure said, 'Mary!'

She knew it was not the gardener, but Jesus himself.

'Rabboni!' she cried, meaning 'Master', and ran to throw her arms around him.

In the days that followed, a great many of Jesus' followers saw him and spoke to him on different occasions before he finally left them and returned to his Father in heaven.

Narrator: So we end our mysterious story. The story of a death, and of a new beginning. It is sometimes hard to understand and to remember something which is mysterious. And so for many years, people have given each other a present on Easter Day as a reminder that on the very first Easter Day, Jesus Christ showed us new life.

That reminder is an Easter egg. Thousands are sold in the shops every Eastertime, and the true reason why we have Easter eggs is because they can remind us of the Easter story.

An egg is rather like a tomb: it is sealed; it looks dead. Yet out of it can come a tiny bundle of life, a new-born chicken. That is why shops sell fluffy chickens at Eastertime. Many Easter cards have eggs and chickens on them.

Out of the egg – the chicken.

Out of the tomb – the living Christ.

Hymn: [*For example, Jesus Christ is Risen Today.*]

Narrator: So Jesus Christ is risen. He came back to life to show us that death is a new beginning, not an end. He is truly alive today.

Prayer: Let us pray

Dear God, soon we shall have the happiness and fun of Easter day and the Easter holidays to enjoy. Help us at this time to remember how Jesus, having died for us on the cross, was raised again alive on the first Easter Sunday morning. Help us not to forget the true meaning of Easter and to remember that Jesus is alive in our hearts every day. Thank you for your great love shown to us. Amen.

Hymn: [*For example, The strife is O'er, or The Day of Resurrection.*]

SECTION 3
Templates,
Timesavers,
Activities,
Resources

Egg templates

75

Template C3

Cockerel template

Template C4

Hen template

Template C5

Easter basket template

Template C6

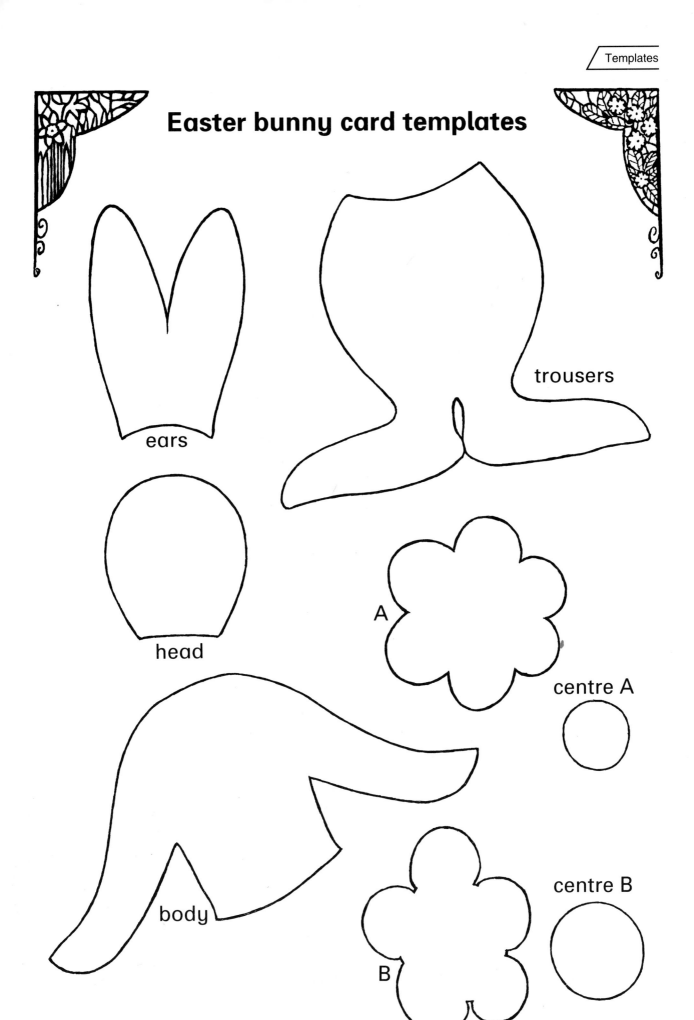

Easter bunny card templates

ears

trousers

head

A

centre A

body

centre B

B

81

Template C9

Swan template

Template C10

Butterfly template

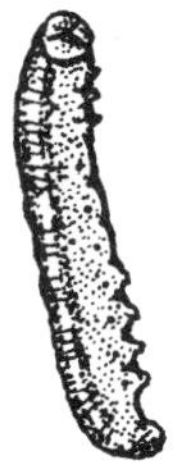

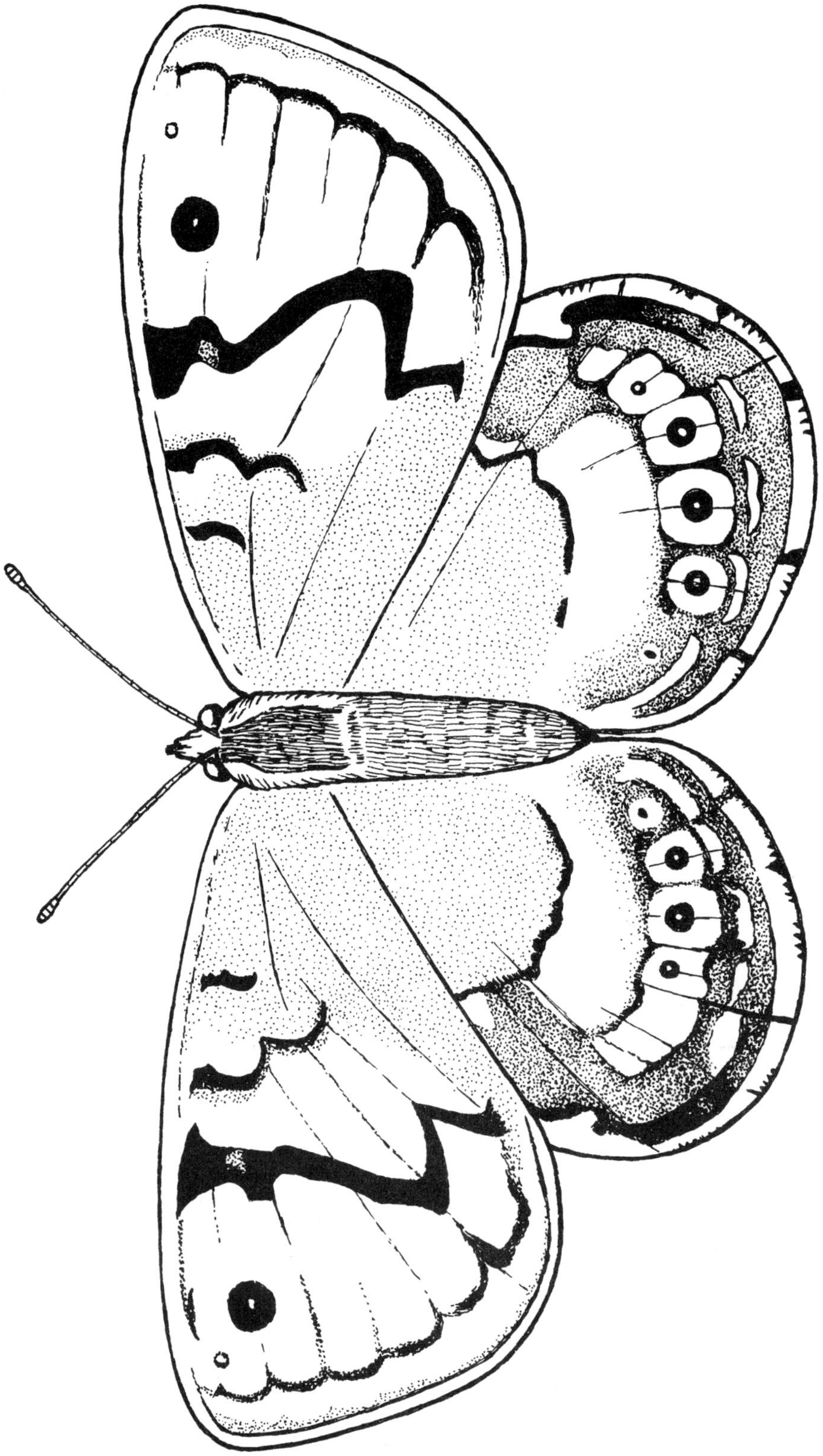

83

Moth template

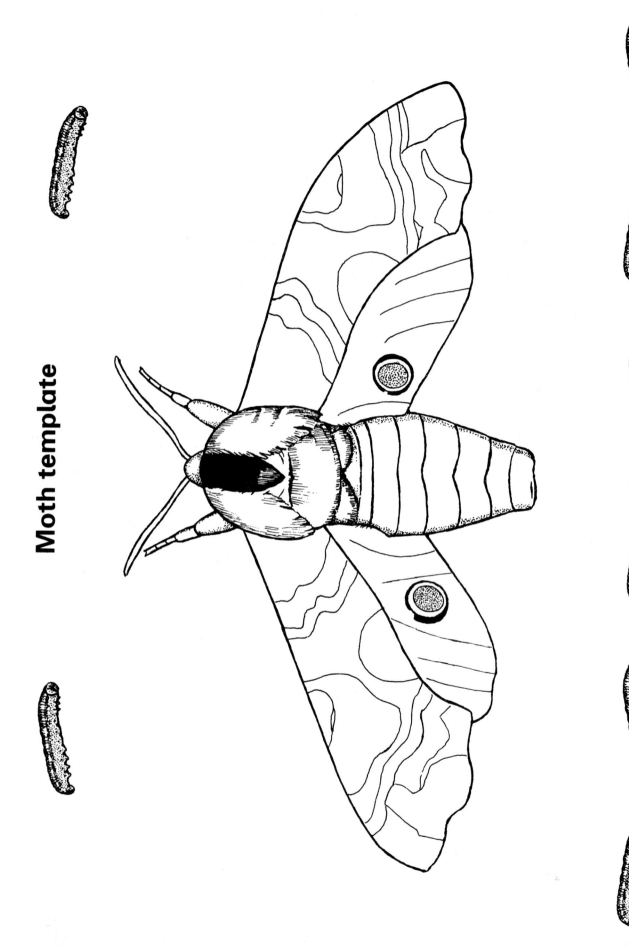

Template C12

Easter lilies template

Template C15

Palm template

Template C16

A calendar for Eastertime

Sun	Mon	Tues	Wed	Thurs	Fri	Sat
		Shrove Tuesday	*Ash Wednesday*			
Palm Sunday				*Maundy Thursday*	*Good Friday*	
Easter Sunday	*Easter Monday*	*Easter Tuesday*				

Template C17

Easter from afar

ANNUAL DOWNTOWN LOS ALTOS

EASTER EGG HUNT

SATURDAY 3 APRIL, 10.00 AM SHARP!

Hunt held in front of stores

Main Street – Ages 1–6

State Street – Ages 7–10

PRIZES!

Over 5 000 eggs filled with candy and gift certificates!

CHILDREN'S ENTERTAINMENT, 10.15 AM (Following Easter egg hunt) ~ Children's show – CitiBank, Corner of State & Main

Rick Rekoon – folk singer

live bunnies

Zany Amy – magician, juggling and unicycling clown

paper hat making

~ Sponsored by the Downtown Los Altos Village Association ~

Template C18

Eastertime fun

Easter charades

Play Easter Charades as a class or in small groups. Sit in a circle. Everyone in turn must act out an Easter topic or custom for the others to identify. Suitable topics include the sun rising, 'heaving', rabbits playing, a chick hatching, people eating hot cross buns, etc. Have some small prizes available for those who guess correctly.

Egg games

A Play pace-egg rolling (see p.104).

B Play 'knock eggs', a traditional Easter game which is often played in Australia on Easter Monday. Each player has one hard-boiled egg. Line up the players in two rows facing each other. Each player holds his or her egg firmly in the fist, so that one end can be seen. Players in one 'attacking' row then knock the ends of the eggs of the players opposite. If the opponent's egg does not break after seven knocks, then it is the turn of the players in the second, 'defending' row to become attackers and attempt to break the eggs of the players in the first row. This goes on, turn and turn about, until one of the eggs breaks. Obviously, the knocker must be careful not to break their own egg by using too much force on their opponent's egg. The winners in each row play against each other, and play-offs continue until one egg – the winning egg – remains intact.

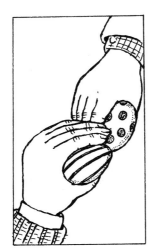

Easter rabbit game

This should be played in the same way as the traditional 'beetle' game. Play in pairs, each competitor having a copy of a rabbit picture sheet. Players take turns to throw a die and may colour in that part of the rabbit corresponding to the number they have thrown: for example, 6 for a head, 5 for an ear, and so on. The first player to colour in the whole rabbit is the winner.

Coloured eggs for breakfast

Dye Easter eggs for breakfast. Hard-boil 6 eggs, add $\frac{3}{4}$ teaspoon of food colouring and 1 teaspoon of vinegar to $\frac{1}{4}$ pint of hot water. Dip eggs until the desired colour is reached. These can of course be eaten as long as eggs are fresh and safe food colouring is used.

91

EASTER RECIPES

Recipes using eggs

A simple quiche   (Serves 4)
1 onion, chopped
2 large tomatoes and 1 green pepper, chopped
25 g cheddar cheese, grated
3 eggs
250 ml ($\frac{1}{2}$ pint) milk
$\frac{1}{2}$ teaspoon salt
$\frac{1}{2}$ teaspoon pepper
20 cm (8") pastry case
1 tablespoon margarine or oil

Gently fry tomatoes, pepper and onion in margarine or oil until softened. Pour off excess liquid and arrange over the base of the pastry case. Sprinkle grated cheese on top. Beat the eggs, and gradually add to them the milk and seasoning. Pour this mixture into the cooked pastry case. Bake at 180°C (350°F, gas mark 4) for 30 to 40 minutes, until set. Serve hot or cold.

Spanish omelette   (Serves 2)
20 ml (1 tablespoon) olive oil
100 g (4 oz) onion, finely chopped
175 g (6 oz) potato, cooked and diced
4 eggs
2 dessertspoons cold water
$\frac{1}{2}$ teaspoon salt
$\frac{1}{2}$ teaspoon pepper

Heat the oil in a small frying pan (omelette pan). Add the onion, and cook gently until soft. Add the potato and cook for 5 minutes. Beat together the eggs, water, salt and pepper. Pour on to the onion mixture. Pull a fork through the mixture to help the egg run through to the base of the pan. Before the omelette is completely set, place under a hot grill. Do not fold this omelette; it should be lifted flat from the pan.

Lemon meringue pie   (Serves 6)
Case and filling
10 to 20 cm (7" to 8") shortcrust pastry flan case – part cooked for 15 minutes at 190°C (375°F, gas mark 5)
3 egg yolks
25 g cornflour
250 ml ($\frac{1}{2}$ pint) water
2 lemons
25 g (1 oz) caster sugar
Meringue topping
2 egg whites
100 g (4 oz)
caster sugar

Blend the cornflour with a tablespoonful of the water. Bring the remainder of the water to the boil and stir in the blended cornflour. Stir until thickened. Boil for two minutes, then remove from heat. Squeeze the juice of lemons and grate their rind. Add to the water and flour mix. Beat in the yolks, one at a time, then the caster sugar. Spread the mixture in the prepared flan case.

Next make the meringue: whisk the egg whites until stiff and dry. Whisk in half the sugar, and gently fold in the other half. Pile the meringue mixture over the filling. Sprinkle some caster sugar on the top. Bake for 45 minutes at 130°C (250°F, gas mark $\frac{1}{2}$) until the meringue is crisp. Serve hot or cold.

Chocolate mousse   (Serves 4)
100 g (4 oz) plain chocolate
200 ml (4 teaspoons) cold water
4 eggs, separated
Chocolate flake or grated chocolate for decoration

Melt all the plain chocolate in water in a basin, over a saucepan of hot water. Remove from the heat when melted. Gradually beat the egg yolks into the melted chocolate. Leave to cool. Whisk the whites, and fold them when stiffened into the chocolate. Pour into small serving dishes. Chill to set. Decorate with chocolate flake or grated chocolate.

Eggs mornay   (Serves 4)
8 eggs, hard-boiled
25 g (1 oz) butter
25 g flour
250 ml ($\frac{1}{2}$ pint) milk
$\frac{1}{2}$ teaspoon salt
$\frac{1}{2}$ teaspoon pepper
100 g (4 oz) cheese, grated

Cut the hard-boiled eggs in half lengthways. Place in an ovenproof dish, the outsides facing downwards. Melt the butter in pan, add the flour and cook for two minutes. Remove from the heat. Stir in the milk and return to the heat, bringing to the boil and stirring until thickened. Add salt and pepper and half of the cheese. Pour the sauce over the eggs. Sprinkle the remaining cheese on top, place under a grill and heat until the cheese is browned.

Mushroom scrambled eggs   (Serves 1)
25 g (1 oz) mushrooms
2 eggs
Pepper and a little salt
15 g ($\frac{1}{2}$ oz) butter
1 slice wholemeal toast

Chop the mushrooms with a knife. Beat the eggs in a bowl with the pepper and salt. Heat the butter in a saucepan, add the mushrooms and cook for a few minutes. Pour the beaten eggs over the mushrooms. Cook slowly, stirring until just set, then carefully remove from the heat and serve with wholemeal toast.

Fairy cakes   (Makes 12)
100 g (4 oz) caster sugar
100 g (4 oz) butter
2 eggs
100 g (4 oz) self-raising flour
Cake decorations or small sweets

Place the cake cases in patty tin holes. Beat the caster sugar and butter together in a mixing bowl until it is fluffy. Beat the eggs in a small bowl using a fork and add them to the sugar and butter mixture a little at a time, beating well after each addition. Fold in the flour using a spoon. Divide the mixture between paper cases using two teaspoons. Use one of the teaspoons to push the mixture off the other teaspoon into the paper cases. Bake for 20 minutes at 190°C (375°F, gas mark 5). Cool on a wire rack. Decorate before serving.

Easter bunny biscuits

2 cups flour
Pinch of salt
1 teaspoon baking soda
1 teaspoon cinnamon
4 oz butter
$\frac{1}{2}$ cup sugar
2 egg yolks
Raisins

Combine the flour, salt, baking soda and cinnamon in a mixing bowl. Beat the sugar, butter and egg yolks in a

biscuit cutter

larger bowl until light and fluffy. Stir in the flour mixture, making a stiff dough. Wrap this in film and chill for several hours. Roll out to 1 cm thickness on a lightly floured surface. Use a bunny-shaped cutter to cut biscuits or make your own cardboard pattern from the shape below. Place biscuits 3 cm apart on lightly greased baking sheets. Use a raisin to make an eye for each rabbit. Bake for 10 to 15 minutes at 350°F (180°C, gas mark 5).

Old country recipes

Fig pudding

Chop finely 8 oz figs and mix with 6 oz grated suet, 4 oz flour and a pinch of salt. Add sufficient milk and beaten eggs to make a stiff dough, then turn into a greased pudding basin and steam for $3\frac{1}{2}$ hours.

Easter cakes

Rub 3 oz butter and 3 oz lard into 3 oz flour. Stir in 1 oz currants, 1 oz chopped peel and 4 oz sugar, and mix to a dough with 2 beaten eggs. Roll the mixture out on a floured board and cut into rounds. Bake in a moderate oven until a pale golden brown.

Cattern cakes

Take 2 lb dough, as made for bread, and knead it well with 2 oz butter or lard, 1 oz caraway seeds, 2 oz sugar and 1 beaten egg. Leave to rise in a warm place for 1 hour, then place in a floured baking tin and bake in a moderate oven.

Note There is a traditional recipe for hot cross buns on p. 103.

Easter fare

EASTER ESSENTIALS ▶

Make a chick egg cosy
You will need:

- yellow and orange felt;
- black beads;

- pins;
- scissors;
- needle and cotton.

Cut out two shapes of template A from the yellow felt.

Cut out the chick's comb and beak from the orange felt, using templates B and C. Place the comb and beak in position on one piece of felt. Place the other piece of felt on top. Pin and then sew together. Sew on beads for the eyes.

cut two

cut two

cut one

cut one

Make palm crosses

Real palm crosses are made from palm leaves. These are obtained from specialist suppliers used by churches, such as Charles Ferris Ltd, Bishopsgate Works, Staines Road, Hounslow, Middlesex. If you are not able to obtain real leaves, light brown coloured card could be used instead. Follow these step-by-step instructions:

Easter brainteasers

Photocopy and distribute **Copymasters 1** to **8** (Easter number puzzle 1–6 and Easter maze 1 and 2) to the class. Let children work individually or in pairs to solve a variety of sticky situations!

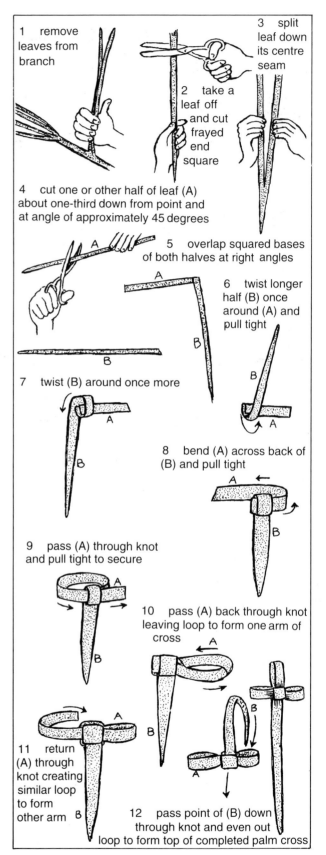

1 remove leaves from branch

2 take a leaf off and cut frayed end square

3 split leaf down its centre seam

4 cut one or other half of leaf (A) about one-third down from point and at angle of approximately 45 degrees

5 overlap squared bases of both halves at right angles

6 twist longer half (B) once around (A) and pull tight

7 twist (B) around once more

8 bend (A) across back of (B) and pull tight

9 pass (A) through knot and pull tight to secure

10 pass (A) back through knot leaving loop to form one arm of cross

11 return (A) through knot creating similar loop to form other arm

12 pass point of (B) down through knot and even out loop to form top of completed palm cross

Easter number puzzle 1

Calculate the following

     +   =

   +   − =

   +  =

   +   =

   + +  =

  − +   =

  +   =

    +   − =

Eastertime fun C1

Easter number puzzle 2

What is the value of the Easter basket in each sum?

$3 \times$ 🧺 $= 6$ 　　　　　 $6 \times$ 🧺 $= 24$

$4 \times$ 🧺 $= 12$ 　　　　 $9 \times$ 🧺 $= 36$

🧺 $\times 5 = 25$ 　　　　 $5 \times 9 =$ 🧺

$3 \times 8 =$ 🧺 　　　　 🧺 $\times 7 = 35$

$10 \times 6 =$ 🧺 　　　 $10 \times$ 🧺 $= 70$

$3 \times 5 =$ 🧺 　　　　 🧺 $\times 3 = 24$

🧺 $\times 9 = 18$ 　　　　 🧺 $\times 11 = 44$

$4 \times$ 🧺 $= 40$ 　　　　 $6 \times$ 🧺 $= 12$

 **Easter number puzzle 3**

Number codes

A	B	C	D	E	F	G	H	I	J	K	L	M
1	2	3	4	5	6	7	8	9	10	11	12	13

N	O	P	Q	R	S	T	U	V	W	X	Y	Z
14	15	16	17	18	19	20	21	22	23	24	25	26

EGG is worth 5 + 7 + 7 = 19

What are these worth?

CHICK

PALM

RABBIT

SUNRISE

LILY

BUN

Easter number puzzle 4

How many eggs are being incubated by each hen?

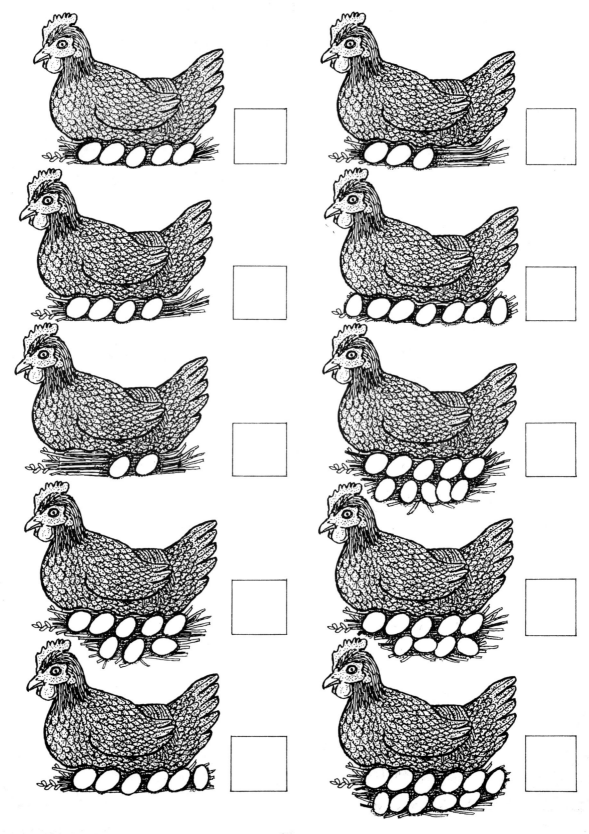

Easter number puzzle 5

Which of these sets can be divided into half?

Which can be divided into thirds?

Which can be divided into quarters?

Eastertime fun C5

Easter number puzzle 6

How many eggs can you count?

Now decorate them all differently.

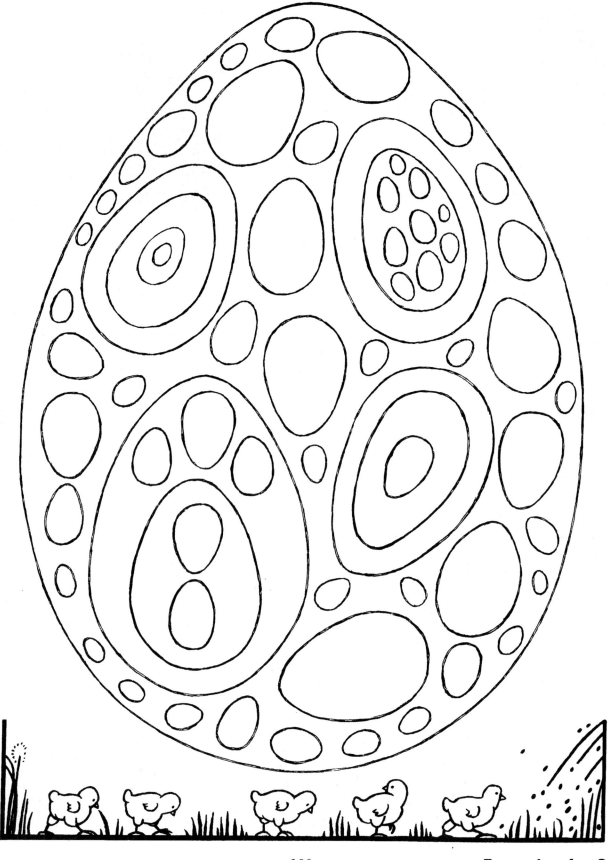

Easter maze 1

Can you help the chick find its mother?

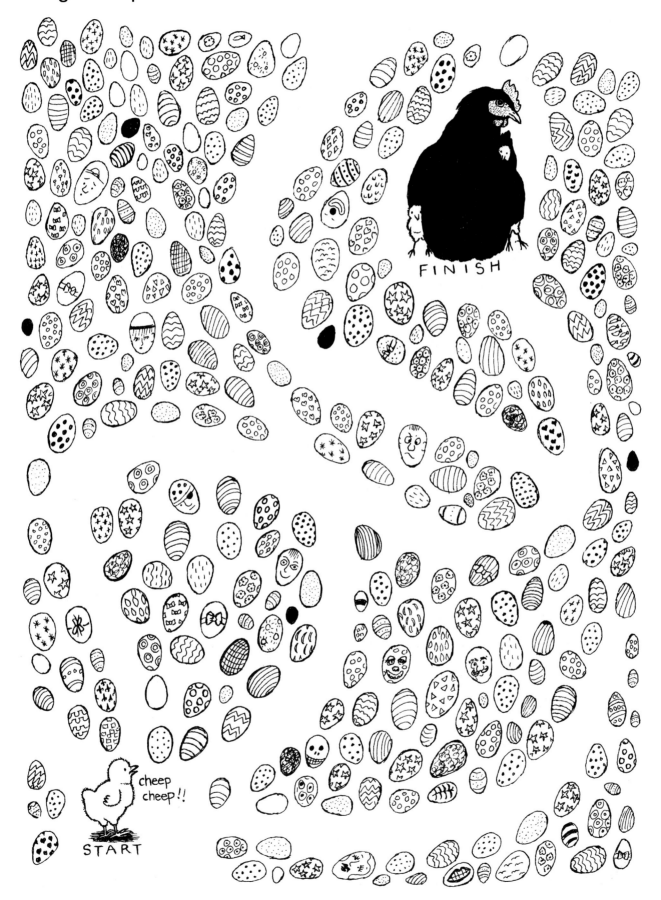

Eastertime fun C7

Easter maze 2

Bunny is lost. Help him to get back to his burrow.

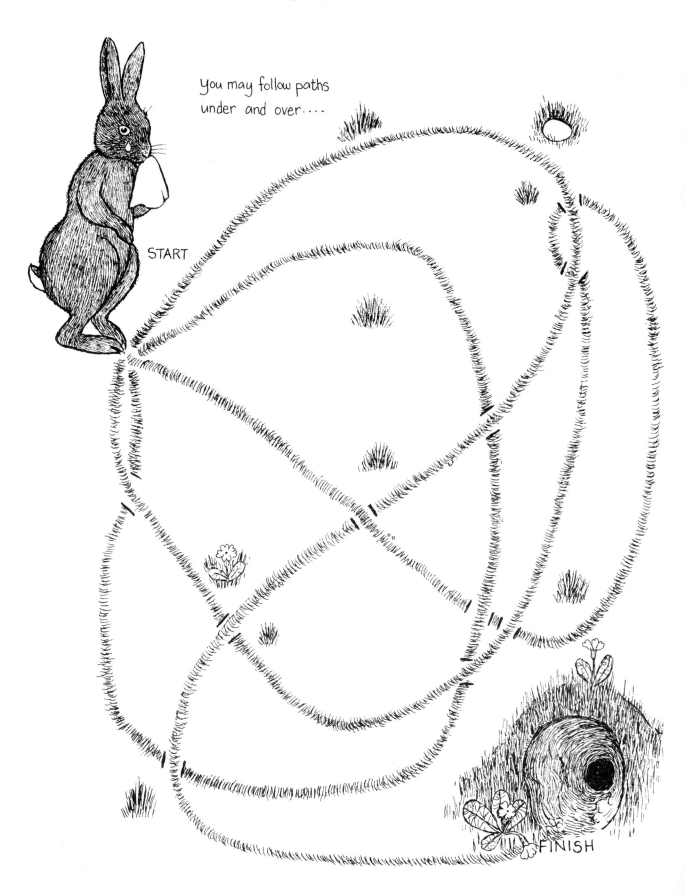

You may follow paths under and over....

START

FINISH

Easter legends and customs

The legend of the dogwood

There is a legend that at the time of the crucifixion the dogwood had been the size of the oak and other forest trees. So firm and strong was the tree that it was chosen as the timber of the cross. To be used thus for such a cruel purpose greatly distressed the tree. Jesus, nailed upon it, sensed this, and in his gentle pity for all sorrow and suffering said to it:

> Because of your regret and pity for my suffering, never again shall the dogwood tree grow large enough to be used as a cross. Henceforth it shall be slender and bent and twisted, and its blossoms shall be in the form of a cross – two long and two short petals. And in the centre of the outer edge of each petal there will be nail prints, brown with rust and stained with red. In the centre of the flower will be a crown of thorns, and all who see it will remember.

Dogwood

Maundy Thursday: a traditional ceremony

On the Thursday before Good Friday, the ceremony of Royal Maundy takes place, usually at Westminster Abbey in London. People from local parishes receive money from the monarch, in the form of silver penny, twopenny, threepenny and fourpenny coins. During the ceremony a Yeoman of the Guard carries a golden tray containing leather purses, some of which are white and some red. There is one purse for each year of the monarch's age. The Maundy Money is in the white purses. In the other purses, there is some ordinary money given instead of the food and clothing that used to be handed out to the poor.

This ceremony has been in existence since the year 1689. Before that, the king or queen went to the Abbey on that day to wash the feet of the poor, in memory of Jesus washing the feet of his disciples during the Last Supper. These Maundy coins are legal tender, but are greatly valued by their recipients, and by collectors. The word 'Maundy' probably comes from the Latin 'mandatum', meaning 'commandment', and referring to the remark, 'A new commandment I give unto you, that ye love one another', made by Jesus during the Last Supper.

The tradition of hot cross buns

Hot cross buns have traditionally been eaten on Good Friday as a reminder of the cross of Christ. Legend tells that these buns would keep for a whole year. In olden days, people often hung them in their homes in the belief that they kept evil spirits away.

A traditional recipe
1 lb (500 g) flour
Pinch salt
1 level teaspoon powdered cinnamon
1 level teaspoon mixed spice
2 oz (25 g) butter
2 oz (25 g) mixed peel
2 oz (25 g) currants
2 oz (25 g) yeast
2 tablespoons caster sugar
$\frac{1}{2}$ pint (250 ml) milk
1 small egg, beaten

Sieve the flour with the salt and spices, rub in the butter and add the currants and mixed peel. Cream the yeast

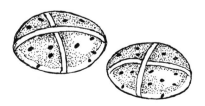

with half of the sugar, add a little warm milk and pour in the centre of the flour. Sprinkle lightly over with flour and leave for 10 minutes. Mix to a stiff dough with the beaten egg, adding a little milk if necessary. Allow to rise until the mixture doubles itself in size. Divide into even portions, mould into small buns and mark with a cross. Place the buns on a greased and floured baking tray. Allow to rise until half as large again. Bake in a hot oven, 220°C (gas mark 7) for 15 minutes. Melt the rest of the sugar in 1 tablespoon of milk and brush over the buns.

Traditions of Good Friday

A variety of customs and superstitions are associated with this day. Some believe it to be an unlucky day (and hence Friday is sometimes thought of as being the unluckiest day of the week, especially when the date is the 13th). This association with bad luck derives from the fact that Jesus was crucified on a Friday. Some people fast or will not eat meat on Good Friday. Fish is a traditional food for Good Friday.

Little work is usually carried out on this day, and many people attend church. For hundreds of years people observed the tradition of carrying out only essential tasks. It is only in very recent years in Britain that some shops and other services have been open and available on this day.

An old country custom is to plant potatoes on Good Friday, because the devil was thought to have no power over the soil on that day. Another superstition is that eating hot cross buns on Good Friday protected one's home from fire.

Often, pace-eggs were given in rural areas on Good Friday, and some people observed the custom of 'creeping to the cross': this custom was popular until the time of Charles II, and involved making rings for the fingers out of the handles or other parts of coffins, which, if consecrated on Good Friday, were believed to protect the wearer from cramp and fits. The consecration of these rings took place during a ceremony known as 'creeping to the cross'.

Pace-egging: an Easter eve custom

An old custom at Eastertime in England involved a ceremony of 'pace-egging'. On Easter eve, boys and men would go to the local towns and villages and perform plays in order to be given gifts such as money and eggs. An ancient rhyme tells of this:

> The next that steps in is old Miser Brown Bags,
> For fear her money she goes in old rags.
> She has gold, she has silver, all laid up in store,
> She's come a-pasche-egging and hopes to get more.

Easter bunny: a tradition

The rabbit or bunny traditionally associated with Easter should actually be a hare. The ancient Egyptians believed that the hare was the symbol of the moon. As we have seen, the date of Easter depends upon the phases of the moon (see p. 6). The hare is also said to be the favourite animal of Eostre, the goddess who gave her name to the festival of Easter. Rabbits have long been established as a symbol of the festival, and are believed to represent love, growth and fertility.

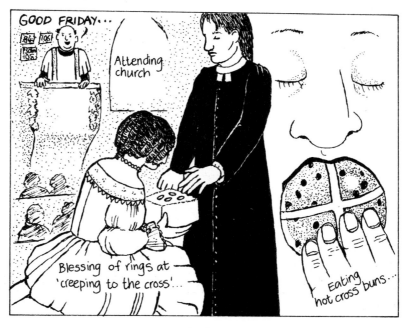

104

Rabbits have long been associated with Easter

eggs would roll down under their own momentum. The original purpose of this game has been lost through the years, but no doubt it was originally associated with a religious ceremony. The eggs were, of course, hard-boiled and the idea was to see whose egg remained unbroken the longest and travelled the furthest.

New clothes for Easter: a tradition
There has long been the tradition of wearing new clothes on Easter Sunday, as a symbol of a new year of life. In some of the major cities of the world, such as New York, there are notable Easter parades, where people walk down the streets (Fifth Avenue in New York) wearing their new clothes. Ladies wear a wonderful assortment of colourful Easter bonnets.

Pace-egg rolling: tradition of Easter Monday
This is an old custom enjoyed by children on Easter Monday. A steep slope was selected for the game, so that

Soul cakes: an Easter Monday custom
In many rural areas, special cakes called soul cakes were made on Easter Monday and given to the poor, who had to sing a song before they could have a cake. Traditional words of one such soul cake song are:

Soul! Soul! for a Soul cake!
I pray you good missis, a Soul cake.
An Apple, a Pear, a Plum or a Cherry,
Or any good thing to make us all merry.
One for Peter, one for Paul,
Three for him that made us all.

Soul cakes

An Easter bonnet parade

'Heaving': a custom for Easter Monday and Tuesday

This custom, known as 'heaving' or 'lifting', dates from three centuries ago in Britain. On Easter Monday, the village men would lift the women up into the air three times, and on Easter Tuesday, the women would do the same to the men. In some villages this was done by holding the legs, while in others people were heaved up on a flower-bedecked chair. It is said that this strange custom was designed to symbolise the resurrection of Jesus Christ.

Easter fun from afar: Los Altos, California

As the poster below indicates, some towns in the USA organise activities for all the children to enjoy at Eastertime.

ANNUAL DOWNTOWN LOS ALTOS

EASTER EGG HUNT

SATURDAY 3 APRIL, 10.00 AM SHARP!

Hunt held in front of stores
Main Street – Ages 1–6
State Street – Ages 7–10

PRIZES!
Over 5 000 eggs filled with candy and gift certificates!

CHILDREN'S ENTERTAINMENT, 10.15 AM (Following Easter egg hunt) ~ Children's show – CitiBank, Corner of State & Main

Rick Rekoon – folk singer

live bunnies

Zany Amy – magician, juggling and unicycling clown

paper hat making

~ Sponsored by the Downtown Los Altos Village Association ~

106

Information and resources

USEFUL ADDRESSES ▶

Equipment (for classroom studies of life cycles)
The Vivarium
55 Boundary Road
Walthamstow
London
E17 8NQ
(For amphibians, reptiles, invertebrates, lighting and
heating equipment and housing.)

Butterfly Farm
Christchurch
14 Grove Road East
Christchurch
Dorset
BH23 2DQ
(For specimens, housing and all resources and
reference material relating to butterflies and moths.)

Entomological Livestock Supplies
Unit 3
Beaver Park
Hayseech Road
Halesowen
West Midlands
B63 3PD
(For foreign and native invertebrates and general
supplies.)

Visual material (for studies of life cycles)
Biological Cycles – a series of wall charts, available
from:
Shell Education Service
Bankside Business Services
10 Fleming Road
Newbury
Berkshire
RG13 2DE

Pictorial Charts Educational Trust
27 Kirchen Road
London
W13 0UD
(For purchase of educational supplies including *The
Variety of Life*; *The Frog* and *Keeping Minibeasts*.)

BOOKS FOR CHILDREN ▶

Back, C. and Olesen, J., *Chicken and Egg*, A & C Black,
   Stopwatch Series
Chinery, M., *All About Baby Animals*, Kingfisher Books
Cox, R. and Cork, B., *Butterflies and Moths*, Usborne,
   First Nature Series
Feltwell, J., *Bugs, Beetles and Other Insects*, Oxford
   University Press
Gee, R., *Babies*, Usborne, Facts of Life Series
Glease, H., *Caterpillars*, Cherry Tree Books
Jennings, T., *Seeds and Seedlings*, Oxford University
   Press, Young Scientist Investigates Series

Kerrod, R., *Plants in Action*, Cherry Tree Books
McGuiness, D. and Rixon, A., *A Child's Book of Animal
   Families*, Hamlyn
Meredith, S., *Where Do Babies Come From?*, Usborne,
   Starting Point Science Series
Morgan, G., *How Things Grow*, Kingfisher Books
Parker, S., *How Nature Works*, Kingfisher Books
Wright, P., *Minibeast*, A & C Black